AF413147

The Mindset Makeover

The Mindset Makeover

5 STEPS TO TRANSFORMING YOUR LIFE

B. Vincent

QuantumQuill Press

Contents

1

Introduction: The Power of Mindset

What Constitutes a Mindset

Constantly influencing each action, decision, and viewpoint is a fundamental and potent force known as the mentality. It serves as the foundation upon which we construct our lives, the filter that imparts color to our experiences, and the lens through which we perceive the world. A mindset is not merely a collection of convictions; it constitutes the fundamental basis of our being, impacting our perceptions of obstacles, responses to hardship, and commemorations of achievements.

One may regard the mindset as an imperceptible architect of one's fate. It influences our actions, which subsequently mold our beliefs, which ultimately mold our reality. This transcends mere optimistic optimism and magical thinking; rather, it signifies the profound realization that the condition of our mind establishes the foundation for the potentialities that arise in our lives. The conviction regarding our capacity for development and progress, as opposed to perceiving ourselves as immutable entities resistant to change, not only influences the trajectory we embark on but also shapes our determination and perseverance in their pursuit.

The ramifications of this are extensive and profoundly individual. A mindset is an intangible quality that permeates all facets of our lives, including our approach to feedback in the workplace, our willingness to undertake risks in the pursuit of our aspirations, and our ability to persevere in the face of obstacles. It affects our approach to learning, the formation of relationships, and even our sense of self-worth.

Gaining an understanding of the fundamental nature of mindset is comparable to discovering the blueprint that governs one's existence. It is recognizing that one must first comprehend and, if necessary, change one's mind before attempting to alter one's existence. This is precisely the purpose of the voyage that this book undertakes. By acknowledging the influence of one's perspective, an inexhaustible array of opportunities becomes accessible. It becomes apparent that a modification in our perspectives, wherein we opt to perceive life from a perspective of development and possibility, has the capacity to revolutionize not only our immediate conditions but our entire being.

As we proceed further into the subsequent pages, bear in mind that the process of altering one's mentality does not entail abandoning one's true self. It is about realizing the tremendous redesigning potential that resides within oneself. It is about transcending a domain of constraints and entering one filled with boundless opportunities. This expedition aims to reveal the fundamental nature of mentality and utilize its potential to fashion a life imbued with meaning, happiness, and satisfaction. Greetings and welcome to the initial stage of this pivotal journey.

Growth vs. Fixed Mindset: The Two Life Paths

A fundamental differentiation between a fixed mindset and a

growth mindset is central to our comprehension of mindset and possesses the potential to fundamentally alter the course of our lives. This notion, which was initially proposed by psychologist Carol Dweck, functions as a strategic guide for traversing the complex path of individual development and success. It serves as a reflection of how we live, learn, and adapt, and is not merely a theory.

A fixed mindset is predicated on the notion that our intellect, talents, and capabilities are immutable characteristics. Individuals who hold this particular perspective perceive themselves as possessing a finite quantity of intelligence or aptitude, a quota that cannot be surpassed through effort. Adhering to this perspective results in an existence that is restricted by perceived constraints. It is a world where criticism is personal and challenges are perceived as threats; effort is reserved for individuals who cannot succeed solely on talent. Because failure represents a direct assault on their identity and self-worth, these individuals frequently prioritize the fear of failure over the pursuit of success.

On the contrary, the growth mindset is one that embraces difficulty with enthusiasm and does not perceive setbacks as indications of inferiority but rather as motivating opportunities for development and the expansion of our current capabilities. This way of thinking is distinguished by the conviction that our fundamental attributes are matters that can be developed through diligent effort. Although individuals may vary in various aspects such as initial talents and aptitudes, interests, and temperaments, it is possible for all to develop and progress through effort and practical experience.

Rather than a desire for approbation, this way of thinking fosters a desire to learn. Its defining characteristic is stubbornness in the face of adversity. Those who exemplify a growth mentality regard effort as the means by which one attains mastery. They recognize that intellectual prowess and talent are merely the foundation upon which their abilities and talents can be built through diligence and effort. This viewpoint cultivates an ardor for acquiring knowledge and an unwavering determination that are both critical for significant achievement. Almost all outstanding individuals have possessed these qualities.

Although transitioning from a fixed to a growth mindset may appear to be traversing a wide chasm, it is more akin to constructing a bridge plank by plank. It pertains to altering our perception of ourselves and our own abilities. It involves recognizing that we are evolving and dynamic rather than inert and unchangeable. This does not imply that with sufficient effort and education, anyone can achieve success. However, this observation suggests that through commitment, mentorship, and determination, it is possible to surpass what we may perceive as our inherent constraints.

By adopting a growth mindset, one goes beyond the conventional pursuit of success. Our goals are development, education, and resiliency. By altering our perception of failure, we come to regard it not as an affirmation of our shortcomings but rather as a beneficial reservoir of expertise and understanding. This way of thinking fails to eradicate obstacles or guarantee effortless achievement. Conversely, it provides us with the outlook and tenacity necessary to successfully traverse the path towards realizing our utmost capabilities.

As we delve into the profound impact that can result from adopting a growth mindset rather than a fixed one, keep in mind that this book is not merely about intellectually comprehending these ideas. It is essential that you internalize them and incorporate them into your daily existence. It is about selecting potential over limitation, learning over inertia, and expansion over stagnation. Greetings and stewards of the growth mindset, where each obstacle serves as an opportunity to advance and the process itself is what matters most.

Effects of One's Mindset on Life's Results

Commencing our exploration of the fundamental influence of mindset on life's results with an awareness of the critical distinction between fixed and development perspectives, we have arrived at this juncture of the inquiry. This narrative transcends scholarly theories and becomes intricately ingrained in the very fabric of our everyday existence. This investigation goes beyond mere observation; it involves actively confronting the concrete, practical repercussions that result from the mindset we elect to embrace.

The silent undercurrent that influences our interactions with the world is our mindset. Analogous to a ship's rudder, although seemingly insignificant in comparison to the immense expanse of the ocean, it effectively guides our entire voyage. The distinction between individuals who possess a growth mindset and those who do not is not inconsequential; rather, it is a paradigm shift.

In the domain of education, not only academic achievement but also a student's approach to learning are determined by their mentality. Individuals who hold a fixed mindset perceive the classroom as a stage where they can exhibit their inherent intellect, and each assessment signifies an acclaim for their immutable capabilities. They are drawn to activities in which they have confidence in their ability to succeed, avoiding difficulties that could reveal their limitations. The apprehension of failing may impede progress, resulting in a cessation of learning and development.

On the contrary, pupils who possess a growth mentality perceive the classroom as a mental gymnasium, where obstacles serve as occasions to fortify their intellectual prowess. They recognize that effort is the driving force behind their accomplishments, and they welcome challenging assignments as opportunities to develop their skills. Their ability to persevere in the midst of obstacles cultivates a more profound and gratifying educational journey, frequently culminating in elevated standards of accomplishment and an ongoing progression of development.

Another vivid illustration of mindset in action is the workplace. Fearing failure, employees with a fixed mindset may refrain from undertaking innovative projects or undertaking new challenges, thereby impeding their professional growth and overall job satisfaction. Individuals might interpret feedback as a form of personal criticism rather than a chance to develop professionally. Conversely, individuals who embrace a growth mindset regard feedback as a valuable opportunity to attain an elevated standard of performance. By actively pursuing difficult projects in order to cultivate their skill set, they exhibit proactive behavior that advances their professional trajectories.

Furthermore, the influence of mindset transcends interpersonal connections. Adopting a fixed mindset may result in an inert perspective towards interpersonal connections, perceiving challenges as immovable barriers. On the contrary, individuals with a growth mindset perceive relationship difficulties as opportunities for personal development and the strengthening of bonds. By utilizing the principles of endeavor and learning to navigate the complexities of interpersonal relationships, they foster stronger and more dynamic bonds.

The influence of one's perspective on the outcomes of life is substantiated by an abundance of empirical research and personal triumphs. It is the story of individuals who, through the application of a growth mindset, triumphed over seemingly insurmountable challenges, rather than relying on pure good fortune or innate ability. Adopting this mentality enables individuals to surpass their own perceived constraints, convert setbacks into learning opportunities, and convert potential into actuality.

In this juncture of decision-making, it is imperative to acknowledge that embracing a growth mindset is not a singular choice, but rather an ongoing journey characterized by a willingness to learn and develop resilience. It involves consciously attempting to transform our internal dialogues from one of stagnation to one of development, from fixed to one of expansion. The consequences of this decision are far-reaching, establishing the foundation for a trajectory replete with development, accomplishment, and a perpetually broadening array of opportunities.

Establishing the Foundation for a Revolution

After conducting an extensive examination of the mindset landscape, which includes a critical differentiation between fixed and growth mindsets and their profound effects on individuals' lives, we have reached a critical juncture: establishing the foundation for personal transformation. This invitation extends beyond a mere academic exercise; it becomes a compelling impetus to initiate one of the most gratifying journeys of your life. It is about acknowledging that the means to achieve one's utmost capabilities is self-aware, and that the process commences with a mental shift.

The mental transformation process is comparable to the preparation of soil for a garden. For growth to occur, it is necessary to have the proper conditions, perseverance, and effort. Recognizing the necessity for change constitutes the initial stage of this procedure. This requires an honest and in-depth examination of our current mindset and its effects on our lives. Are we constrained by the limitations of a fixed mentality, wherein we perceive our capabilities as immutable and static? Is there a beginning indication of the emergence of a growth mindset, wherein individuals acknowledge their capacity for learning and progress?

The next stage, after recognizing the necessity for change, is to comprehend that transformation is feasible. At this juncture, the influence of belief becomes apparent. Preserving a positive outlook on change is the foundation upon which a garden of transformation is constructed. It entails recognizing that while our present mindset has been influenced by environmental factors, heredity, and past experiences, it is not immutable. The biological foundation for altering our mentality is the phenomenon of neuroplasticity, which explains the brain's extraordinary capacity for change.

In order to prepare for this transformation, we must establish precise, deliberate objectives. Which facets of our mentality do we desire to modify? Is it our mindset toward obstacles, our response to setbacks, or our confidence in our capacity for development? Determining precise and practical objectives provides direction for an endeavor, designating significant stages that we strive to attain.

Creating an environment conducive to growth is of equal significance. This entails establishing connections with individuals who exemplify the growth mindset, actively searching out educational and motivational resources, and developing routines that strengthen our resolve to undergo personal change. Establishing a support network that provides encouragement during times of weakness and acknowledges achievements throughout the process is crucial.

In conclusion, establishing the foundation for change entails approaching the process with forbearance and empathy. Change is not an overnight process. Time, persistence, and a readiness to confront the unease that frequently accompanies development are essential. Self-compassion is essential, as it entails acknowledging that setbacks are not indications of failure, but rather prospects for growth and learning.

As we commence this endeavor of mental transformation, it is critical to bear in mind that this pursuit is not an individual one. By providing insights, strategies, and exercises intended to facilitate your development, this book functions as your guide. In this collaborative effort, we shall examine the pragmatic measures that can be taken to foster a growth mentality, surmount challenges, and ultimately effectuate a profound metamorphosis in one's life.

The trajectory is well-defined and the stage is prepared. It is now appropriate to initiate the initial phase of a profound introspective metamorphosis. With a receptive attitude and a determined spirit, accept the challenge at hand, for the ensuing expedition possesses the capability to transform not only your perspective, but your entire existence. Embrace the profound influence of one's mentality, where each progressive action contributes to the development of a more complete and empowered individual.

Preparation for the Upcoming Journey

As we approach a critical juncture, having examined the fundamental nature of mindset, distinguished between fixed and growth perspectives, acknowledged their significant consequences, and established the foundation for individual transformation, we are presently prepared to commence the forthcoming expedition. This concluding portion of our introduction functions as a preparatory and illuminating element, prompting you to wholeheartedly embark on the transformative journey with bravery, purpose, and receptiveness.

Commencing this endeavor necessitates not merely comprehension of the principles expounded in the antecedent segments; rather, it demands a proactive and invested dedication to implementing these insights in one's day-to-day existence. Transformation is an active endeavor, requiring a continuous series of decisions to be made on a moment-by-moment basis. To adequately equip oneself for the forthcoming expedition, contemplate the subsequent obligations:

Adopt an Attainment of Transparency: Commence this expedition with a receptive mindset and sentiment. Be open to questioning and challenging deeply ingrained convictions concerning oneself and the surrounding world. Openness serves as the fertile ground where the seeds of transformation are planted, facilitating expansion and alteration that were previously deemed unattainable.

Embrace Vulnerability: The process of transformation entails the examination of concealed or evaded aspects of one's being. It necessitates confronting one's fears, accepting one's vulnerabilities, and being candid regarding one's aspirations and ambitions. Vulnerability does not indicate frailty; rather, it signifies a courageous and strong position that facilitates authentic transformation.

Develop Resilience: The journey towards altering one's mindset will undoubtedly encounter various obstacles. Delays and periods of uncertainty are inevitable. Critical is the development of resilience —the capacity to recover from adversity. It requires the ability to perceive challenges as chances for personal development, deriving knowledge from each encounter, and maintaining focus on over-arching objectives at all times.

Engage in the practice of self-compassion by maintaining a kind attitude toward oneself during this endeavor. The process of change can be challenging, and self-criticism can pose a significant obstacle. Engage in the practice of self-compassion by engaging in mindful, considerate, and patient self-talk. Acknowledge that progress does not follow a linear trajectory, and commemorate each incremental win as a triumph deserving of jubilation.

Persist in Your Engagement: Transformation demands ongoing dedication and active participation. This practice entails the pro-active implementation of growth mindset principles across multiple domains, encompassing personal aspirations as well as professional complexities. Maintain motivation and inspiration throughout your journey by establishing consistent self-check-ins, modifying your strategies as necessary, and consistently seeking out resources and support.

As you readily anticipate embarking on this transformative voyage, bear in mind that you are not alone. This book serves as a companion, providing guidance, exercises, and insights that are intentionally crafted to assist the reader at each stage. By committing to a mentality shift, the community of fellow aspirants and the experiences of those who have traversed this path before you serve as poignant reminders of the potential that exists.

Anticipated is a voyage of self-discovery, development, and empowerment. This path not only results in a mental transformation, but also a complete metamorphosis of one's existence. As you progress, you will gradually reveal additional facets of your capabilities, develop the ability to confront life's obstacles with poise and perseverance, and ultimately, come to terms with the limitless opportunities that emerge from adopting a growth mindset.

Welcoming you on this voyage. Although initially challenging, that first action is always the most rewarding. Accept the endeavor with a receptive mindset, and permit the metamorphosis to commence.

2

Chapter 1: Recognizing Your Current Mindset

Recognizing Restricted Beliefs

Beliefs that define a mindset are as fundamental to it as the framework that establishes the boundaries and form of a house. Limiting beliefs are especially pernicious among these, functioning as imperceptible obstacles that impede our development and potential. These are the profoundly ingrained convictions that frequently masquerade as indisputable realities concerning our capacities, value, and potential accomplishments in life. There are those who murmur that our capabilities are limited, that we are incapable of exceeding certain limits, or that our aspirations are excessively ambitious for an individual of our caliber.

The process of transformation commences with the identification of these concealed saboteurs. The act of uncovering these beliefs from the depths of our consciousness necessitates a readiness to do so. This procedure emphasizes self-awareness rather than self-evaluation. It is acknowledging that these beliefs are not fundamental to our being; instead, they are external influences such as societal pressures, past experiences, or the advice of trustworthy individuals.

Identify your limiting beliefs by focusing on situations in which you have encountered persistent obstacles or where you feel trapped. These domains are frequently governed by limiting beliefs. Consider the narratives that you narrate to yourself, paying particular attention to those that commence with "I cannot," "I am not," or "I do not." These assertions serve as indicators, morsels that guide you back to the fundamental convictions that establish the limits of your perceived capabilities.

Consider the following common limiting beliefs:

"I'm not smart enough to achieve my dreams."

"I don't have the talent to succeed in my field."

"I'm too old (or too young) to start something new."

"It's selfish to pursue my own happiness."

"Making mistakes means I'm a failure."

The act of recognizing these beliefs demands bravery. It involves acknowledging and confronting the shadows that have formed a portion of us due to fear, failure, or criticism. It is, however, the initial stride towards emancipation. We deprive our limiting beliefs of the ability to dictate our actions and decisions unconsciously by naming them.

After identifying these beliefs, record them. Engaging in the process of visualizing these beliefs in black and white can serve as a potent externalization exercise, prompting one to acknowledge that they are not inherent truths but rather acquired perceptions susceptible to modification. Engaging in the practice of writing serves as an initial stride towards reclaiming one's agency, signifying one's readiness to scrutinize the underpinnings of one's present world-view and replace them with fresh, empowering convictions.

Keep in mind that recognizing your limiting beliefs is a beginning, not a conclusion. It signifies the commencement of a transformative journey culminating in a more genuine, satisfying, and boundless being. Exercising self-compassion and perseverance is recommended as you advance in this endeavor. Although transformation requires time, each progressive step signifies an escape from constraints and a descent into the realm of potentiality.

Comprehending the Effects

After illuminating our limiting beliefs and bringing them to the forefront of our conscious awareness, the subsequent critical course of action is to confront the profound influence they have on our existence. These convictions, which are frequently embraced inadvertently and without explicit assent, permeate the very fabric of our being, impacting judgments, molding actions, and tingling our perspectives regarding ourselves and the external environment. In order to embark on the path to transformation, it is essential that we not only recognize these beliefs but also comprehend their extensive and profound impact.

Restricted beliefs function as veils by which our successes, failings, and experiences are perceived and understood. They have the ability to transform challenges into formidable barriers and opportunities into dangers. The conviction that "I lack the intelligence to attain my aspirations" can impede the pursuit of educational opportunities, the attempt at novel experiences, and the application for jobs that appear impracticable. It is a self-fulfilling prophecy when the very actions that could lead to success are averted by the dread of failure or inadequacy.

The ramifications of these convictions transcend individual development and success; they influence interpersonal connections, professional trajectories, and general welfare. A belief such as "I do not deserve to be loved" can cause us to accept less than we truly deserve or to undermine connections that offer us the affection and regard we subconsciously believe we are not deserving of. From a professional standpoint, harboring the conviction that "I am incapable of achieving success in my field" could impede our progress, deprive us of fulfillment, and prevent us from actively seeking mentorship, pursing promotions, or contributing novel ideas.

In order to comprehend the ramifications of limiting beliefs, one must acknowledge the behavioral patterns that they generate. Such ingrained patterns may contribute to our self-acceptance, leading us to fail notice that they are merely external constraints that have the capacity to be modified. It is imperative to trace the origins of these patterns in order to comprehend how they have impacted the course of our lives and to recognize the toll that their influence has taken.

This realization signifies an act of empowerment rather than an exercise in self-reproach. Through recognizing the consequences of our limiting beliefs, we can initiate the process of untying ourselves from their sway. We begin to perceive the potential for choice in situations where none appeared previously. It is widely acknowledged that individuals possess the ability to reshape their lives in accordance with their genuine desires and aspirations, to interpret their experiences in a different light, and to make decisions that are in line with their true potential.

In order to fully comprehend the ramifications of your limiting beliefs, contemplate the subsequent inquiries:

In what ways have my prior decisions and actions been influenced by these beliefs?

To what extent have they impeded my pursuit of challenges or opportunities?

In what ways have they impacted my personal development, professional progress, and interpersonal connections?

In what ways have they affected my sense of self-worth and self-esteem?

Gaining insight into the consequences of one's self-imposed limitations is an essential stride towards liberation. The concept pertains to perceiving the chains for what they truly are—impassable barriers that demand cognizance, deliberate effort, and implementation to surmount. As you progress along this path, bear in mind that the capacity to effectuate a life-altering transformation resides not in modifying external conditions, but in reconfiguring the internal terrain of one's convictions. This comprehension is crucial in order to access a future that is not constrained by the past; it is a future in which one determines their own fate.

Engaging in Self-Reflection Activities

After shedding light on the obscure areas where constraining beliefs exist and recognizing their significant influence on our existence, we now progress to the domain of proactive change. Explorational tools are necessary for this inward voyage; self-reflection exercises function as both a compass and a map. The purpose of these exercises is not only to challenge our limiting beliefs, but also to comprehend them and, ultimately, to reframe their narrative.

1. Reflection of Writing:
   The initial task prompts you to partake in the transformative process of composition. Writing for oneself rather than for an audience constitutes an intimate conversation with one's most profound truths. List your identified limiting beliefs to begin. Please provide an example of how each of these beliefs affected a decision or action next to it. This process of correlation serves to concretize the intangible, demonstrating how these convictions have influenced the trajectory of your existence.

2. The Reversal of Roles:

To gain perspective, you will step outside of yourself during this exercise. Envision that a close companion confides in you, articulating the very self-recognized limiting beliefs that you have acknowledged. Should you mention anything to them? What advice would you give them? Please compose your reply. By employing empathy and compassion, which are frequently more accessible towards others than towards ourselves, this exercise attempts to confront and ameliorate these severe convictions.

3. Digging Historical:

We examine the origins of these beliefs in this section. Assign each limiting belief to the earliest memory of experiencing such emotions. Was it a parental message, a remark made by the student, or an instance of individual inadequacy? Gaining insight into the origins of these beliefs can assist in debunking their influence, unveiling them as acquired patterns rather than intrinsic verities.

4. The Reality Assessment:

Engaging in this exercise entails questioning the soundness of one's limiting beliefs. Engage in introspection regarding each personal belief by posing the following question: "Can I conceive of any instances that contradict this belief? "This approach, which draws inspiration from cognitive-behavioral techniques, fosters the cultivation of a more nuanced understanding of our self-imposed constraints grounded in empirical evidence.

5. Prospective Scripting:

Finally, conceive of an existence in which these limiting beliefs do not bind you. Compose an elaborate account of an ideal day, week, or year devoid of the aforementioned limitations. What emotions would you experience? What are your intended pursuits?

By allowing yourself to fully realize the potential of a life governed by empowering beliefs, this exercise is not about fantasy.

Engaging in self-reflection exercises is not a singular endeavor; rather, it entails ongoing cultivation and improvement. They function as instruments for excavation, construction, and shaping a mindset that fosters personal development and ambition. Approach these exercises with benevolence and tolerance as you participate. Recall that the objective is not critique, but rather comprehension, and transformation occurs through comprehension.

Engaging in self-reflection is a complex and gratifying process. It demands that we confront previously evaded aspects of ourselves, but it also presents the potential for personal emancipation. Through active participation in these exercises, one not only challenges their limiting beliefs but also establishes the foundation for a significant personal transformation. This is the substance of transformation: becoming the person that one is destined to be through a deliberate, reflective process, as opposed to a sudden metamorphosis.

Techniques for Awareness and Mindfulness

Equipped with the knowledge gained from our self-reflection endeavors, we now redirect our focus towards developing a state of mindfulness and consciousness. The intersection of the theory of transformation and everyday existence occurs at this juncture. Mindfulness and awareness techniques transcend mundane relaxation or concentration exercises; they constitute fundamental practices that enable individuals to impartially and lucidly observe their thoughts and beliefs. By cultivating a mindful attitude toward our thoughts, we can begin to distinguish our limiting beliefs from ourselves, thereby creating an opportunity for transformation and development.

1. The Habitus of Being Present:

Mindfulness commences with the cultivation of presence—becoming entirely engrossed in the present moment. This practice consists of daily, straightforward exercises like mindful dining, focused breathing, and walking meditation. The objective is to develop into an observer of one's thoughts, recognizing them without emotion or judgment, rather than striving to empty one's consciousness. The elevated level of consciousness affords an alternative viewpoint on the automatic thought processes that underpin our restrictive convictions.

2. A Masterwork of Observation:

   The next stage, after one has initiated the process of developing presence, is to engage in the skill of observation. This practice entails consistently monitoring one's thoughts and emotions, particularly in circumstances that elicit the activation of limiting beliefs. Through careful observation of the ways in which these beliefs impact one's reactions and decisions, one can initiate the process of unraveling themselves from their sway. The crucial factor is to observe without passing judgment, recognizing that mere awareness is a potent catalyst for transformation.

3. The Methodology of Labeling:

   One efficacious strategy within the repertoire of mindfulness practices is the method of labeling. Mentally designate a limiting belief as such when you become aware of its emergence; it is not a fact. As an illustration, label the following thought: "I lack the competence to achieve success" or "I have a limiting belief." This elementary action of assigning a label to the thought establishes a mental distance from it, diminishing its immediate influence and affording the opportunity to scrutinize its soundness.

4. An Application of Gratitude:

By incorporating the practice of gratitude into one's daily routine, attention can be redirected from perceived deficiencies to the ample resources that are presently manifesting in one's life. Spend a few moments each day listing three things for which you are appreciative. Engaging in this practice serves the dual purpose of promoting mindfulness and challenging the scarcity mentality that frequently forms the basis of limiting beliefs.

5. The Compassionate Inquiry Path:

In conclusion, adopt the stance of compassionate inquiry. This entails curiously and benevolently challenging your limiting beliefs in a gentle manner. Consider the following: "From what threat does this belief seek to shield me?" or "Is there an alternative perspective that is more empowering in nature?" Compassionate inquiry enables one to examine the origins and consequences of one's beliefs without evaluative self-interest, thereby cultivating a more profound comprehension and facilitating the process of personal growth.

Awareness and mindfulness are not merely practices; they are methods of being in the world. They enable us to approach life with enhanced clarity, tranquility, and purpose. Through the adoption of these practices, we bestow upon ourselves the necessary resources to gracefully traverse the path of transformation. By overcoming the influence of our limiting beliefs, we develop the ability to live in accordance with our most profound truths and loftiest ambitions. This paradigm shift signifies not the conclusion of the expedition, but rather an inception into a realm where our thoughts and convictions serve as allies, steering us in the direction of our utmost capabilities.

A synopsis and appeal for action

As we approach the conclusion of the initial chapter, "Recognizing Your Current Mindset," we have undertaken a pivotal voyage of introspection. By recognizing and acknowledging our limiting beliefs, comprehending the wide-ranging consequences of these beliefs, conducting introspection, and developing mindfulness and awareness, we have established the foundation for significant individual growth and change. This final segment functions as both a recapitulation of our progress thus far and a strong impetus to proceed, encouraging you to implement the knowledge and strategies into your everyday existence.

Acknowledging one's present mindset is comparable to turning on a lamp in a chamber that has been dark for an extended period of time. It sheds light on the concealed facets of one's belief system, unveiling both the unexplored potential that lies within and the constraining beliefs that have impeded progress. The exercises and techniques discussed in this chapter serve as valuable resources for uncovering and refining concealed treasures, removing debris and enhancing their brilliance to illuminate the path ahead.

The Strength of Acknowledgment:

Never forget that acknowledging your present mindset possesses an immense amount of power. It is an essential initial step in the direction of change. Any attempt at transformation in the absence of this fundamental comprehension is akin to constructing a home on unstable ground. Through the identification and comprehension of one's limiting beliefs, one initiates the procedure of establishing a robust groundwork for subsequent endeavors.

The odyssey of introspection:

The provided exercises for self-reflection are intended to be reviewed again. Transformation is an ongoing process of development and acquisition of knowledge, not a singular occurrence. With each iteration of these exercises, you will gradually reveal additional depths of comprehension pertaining to yourself and your convictions. It is deserving of your kindness, perseverance, and patience on this voyage.

The Application of Awareness and Mindfulness:

On this voyage, mindfulness and awareness serve as companions. They infuse the process with tranquility and clarity, enabling one to impartially observe one's thoughts and beliefs. These practices serve as more than mere instruments for acknowledging one's limiting beliefs; they impart enduring abilities that improve one's overall welfare, capacity for happiness, and resilience.

A Request for Action:

I would like to conclude this chapter by addressing a call to action. Implement what you have recently acquired. Commence each day by performing a mindfulness exercise, persist in engaging in introspection, and employ compassionate inquiry to confront your limiting beliefs. As you incorporate these practices into your daily regimen, you will notice a noticeable transformation in the terrain of your psyche.

Keep in mind that the path you are traversing is profoundly individual and unlike any other. There will be instances of profound insight and moments of doubt, as well as setbacks and breakthroughs. Maintain the conviction that by altering your perspective, you are gaining access to a life filled with increased satisfaction, meaning, and happiness.

While progressing to the subsequent chapter, retain the knowledge and insights gained thus far. Peruse the subsequent phases of your transformation while remaining steadfast on the foundation laid by them. The forthcoming trajectory is replete with potentialities, and you have acquired the necessary knowledge and abilities to traverse it with sophistication and purpose. You have already commenced your transformative journey and are well on your way to becoming the most self-assured and genuine it is possible to be.

With courage, inquiry, and an open heart, proceed. Your ideal future is not merely conceivable; it is eagerly awaiting your efforts to manifest it.

3

Chapter 2: Cultivating Self-Awareness

Consideration of Self-Awareness

Within the expansive fabric of individual growth, self-awareness serves as the unifying element that binds our cognition, sentiments, and behaviors with the assurance of comprehension. It serves as an illuminated mirror that is raised above our interior world, reflecting not only our current selves but also our future selves. Chapter 1 commences by examining the critical significance of self-awareness in the process of individual metamorphosis, thereby establishing the foundation for a more profound investigation into our selves and the external environment.

Fundamentally, self-awareness pertains to the deliberate understanding of an individual's own disposition, emotions, drives, and aspirations. It is the capacity to perceive one's own reflections with clarity, comprehending one's own strengths and limitations, thought processes, and emotional reactions. However, its significance transcends simple self-reflection. Self-awareness serves as the fundamental underpinning behind our potential for development, transformation, and fortitude. It enables us to live with authenticity and integrity, to align our actions with our innermost values, and to navigate the complexities of life with purpose and direction.

Can you conceive of traversing the immense oceans in a ship without the aid of a compass or a map? Such is the trajectory of existence devoid of self-awareness. Although we may advance, driven by the currents of events, our course of action remains ambiguous and our ultimate aim is not certain. Self-awareness equips us with the navigational tool and strategic plan required to determine our path, discern the forces that influence us, and navigate through both turbulent and tranquil conditions.

Establishing and nurturing self-awareness constitutes the initial phase in a mental paradigm shift. It compels individuals to critically examine their thoughts and actions, to scrutinize the foundations of their convictions, and to confront the anxieties and uncertainties that impede progress. We thereby expose ourselves to the potential for transformation. We begin to perceive the disparities between our current selves and our desired selves not as insurmountable barriers, but rather as opportunities for personal development.

Furthermore, self-awareness enhances interpersonal connections. It enhances our capacity for effective communication, profound empathy, and adept conflict resolution. By developing an awareness of our own emotions and responses, we enhance our capacity to comprehend those of others, thereby promoting the formation of relationships founded on mutual regard and comprehension.

The pursuit of heightened self-awareness is not devoid of obstacles. In order to develop, it is often necessary to muster the fortitude to confront one's own imperfections and susceptibilities, as well as to welcome the unease that accompanies this process. However, the benefits are incalculable. As we progress, we develop a more profound comprehension of our own selves, establish a more robust framework for our lives, and attain a more lucid outlook on the trajectory that awaits us.

In the following sections of this chapter, we shall examine pragmatic approaches to augmenting emotional intelligence, the profound impact that journaling can have on personal growth, and the significance of feedback loops in fostering self-awareness. You will find these practices and tools to be your allies on the path to a more empowered, conscious, and fulfilled existence.

By adopting self-awareness, individuals initiate a continuous process of self-exploration, intellectual development, and progress. This path not only facilitates self-awareness but also fosters a more profound connection with the external environment. Let us progress with receptive hearts and inquisitive minds, prepared to delve into the profundities of our beings and to liberate the complete potential of our existence.

The quality of emotional intelligence

While endeavouring to develop self-awareness, we come across an influential companion known as emotional intelligence (EQ), which significantly influences our engagements with both ourselves and others. This chapter provides an in-depth analysis of EQ, separating its constituent parts and illustrating how augmenting it can result in a more reflective, compassionate, and resilient way of being. Emotional intelligence serves as the conduit that links our cognizance of our internal realm with our understanding of interpersonal connections and societal interactions.

Four fundamental components comprise emotional intelligence: self-awareness, self-regulation, empathy, and social abilities. Every individual pillar functions as a fundamental element, providing assistance and enhancing our ability to comprehend and traverse our own emotional terrain as well as that of others.

Being Self-Aware:

Self-awareness is the initial step; it is the capacity to identify and comprehend one's own emotions. This is the reflective surface by which we behold our deepest emotions, aspirations, and anxieties. This pertains to the recognition of our emotional impulses, comprehension of the underlying causes of our emotions, and awareness of the influence that our emotions exert on our cognition and behavior. This profound self-awareness is the initial stride in conquering our emotional states as opposed to allowing them to control us.

Self-regulation entails

Self-awareness is intricately connected to self-regulation, which pertains to the capacity to effectively control and guide one's emotions in a constructive and suitable manner. The cultivation of self-control entails pausing prior to reacting, selecting responses that are consistent with one's values and objectives, as opposed to succumbing to impulsive emotions. Self-regulation enables individuals to effectively manage obstacles and make choices that are beneficial to their overall welfare in the long run.

A sense of empathy:

In accordance with the third pillar, empathy expands our emotional comprehension to include others. It is the ability to empathize with another individual, experience their emotions, and perceive the world through their lens. Empathy facilitates interpersonal connections by cultivating profound comprehension, compassion, and bonding. Cultivating relationships, resolving conflicts, and fostering inclusive environments where all individuals feel valued and comprehended are all aspects that require this skill.

Social Abilities:

Emotional intelligence ultimately reaches its pinnacle in social skills, which encompass the capacity to adeptly navigate social situations, engage in fruitful communication, and establish and sustain positive relationships. These abilities empower us to articulate our thoughts with precision and assurance, to engage in active listening, and to cooperate with others in pursuit of shared objectives. Proficient social abilities elevate both our personal and professional spheres, providing access to novel prospects and fostering more meaningful exchanges with others.

Improving our emotional intelligence necessitates an ongoing commitment to development and education, rather than a nightly endeavor. The process commences with an earnestness to engage in introspection and personal growth, a readiness to confront our weaknesses, and a commitment to exhibiting empathy and comprehension in our social exchanges.

To enhance one's emotional intelligence, the following practices may be contemplated:

Consider your emotional reactions to a variety of situations. What precipitates them? In what ways do they influence your beliefs and actions?

By cultivating mindfulness, one can enhance their ability to regulate themselves. Engaging in mindfulness exercises can enhance one's self-awareness of their emotions, thereby providing the opportunity to deliberate on their reactions.

Embrace a variety of viewpoints in order to enhance your capacity for empathy. Analyze narratives, personal experiences, and opposing points of view.

Master the art of communication. Active listening, straightforward communication, and constructive criticism should be practices.

Developing and improving one's emotional intelligence leads to the attainment of heightened self-awareness, enhanced capacity for connection, and increased resilience. In addition to being a valuable tool for traversing the intricacies of social interactions, EQ is an essential element in maintaining a satisfying and harmonious existence. Developing our emotional intelligence fosters a greater sense of consciousness, empathy, and interconnectedness in our lives.

The Strength of a Journal

As we further examine the significance of self-awareness in facilitating personal growth and change, we shall now employ a method of profound simplicity and profundity: journaling. Engaging in this routine, which is frequently disregarded amidst the frenzy of everyday existence, serves as an entrance to the depths of our being, a mirror reflecting with astonishing clarity the nuances of our thoughts, emotions, and experiences. Engaging in the practice of journaling transcends mere writing; it entails an intimate conversation with one's psyche, serving as a vehicle to navigate personal development, comprehend emotional terrain, and express profound aspirations.

Critical Elements of Journaling:

The act of keeping a journal provides an exceptional environment—an intimate and unbiased setting in which one can candidly articulate their thoughts and emotions. Engaging in the practice of writing extends beyond the simple recording of occurrences; it constitutes a journey of revelation, exploration, and occasionally the restoration of aspects of oneself. By maintaining a journal, we can discern our emotional triggers, monitor our thought patterns, and clarify our aspirations and objectives. Engaging in this activity consistently fosters a profound sense of self-awareness, enabling us to assess our progress and identify our future aspirations.

Positive aspects of journaling include:

The advantages of maintaining a journal are numerous. Facilitating the expression of frustrations and concerns in a secure and constructive environment, it functions as a stress-relieving instrument. It facilitates a heightened sense of introspection, elevating our consciousness of our internal conditions and enabling us to identify and comprehend our emotions. In addition to enhancing our problem-solving and creative capacities, journaling fosters novel ideas and concepts, which frequently result in realizations and resolutions that evade our notice amidst the clamor of daily existence.

Commencing Your Journaling Routine:

A journaling practice necessitates only a notebook and a pen, but the true dedication lies in maintaining consistency and being truthful. Listed below are some guidelines to assist you in getting started:

Make a conscious decision regarding the format: Whether it be an elegantly bound notebook or a digital document, opt for a medium that evokes a sense of ease and accessibility.

Establish a routine: Write in your journal at a specific time each day or week. The adherence to this routine transforms the activity into a sacred moment of introspection.

Allow yourself to write freely, disregarding worries regarding grammar or style. Journaling serves as a personal space where one should freely express thoughts and emotions, free from the constraint of self-criticism.

Engage in introspection: Record your daily interactions, the emotions you encountered, and the thoughts that plagued your mind in your journal. Consider themes that recur or patterns.

Employ self-inquiry: Consult your inner self through the use of a journal. What gives me pleasure? What precisely do I fear? What are the depths of my desires? These inquiries have the potential to unveil additional strata of comprehension and longing.

Constructing a Journaling System Into Your Journey:

As you incorporate journaling into your process of developing self-awareness, you will discover that it transcends being a mere exercise and instead becomes a companion. The journal serves as a chronicle of one's development, a solace for uncertainties, and a medium for manifesting aspirations. It is capable of changing thoughts into words, which in turn can inspire actions. As time passes, the entries in your journal will transform into a tangible reminder of your voyage toward a more profound and interconnected sense of self, serving as a roadmap of your personal development.

When striving to develop self-awareness, journaling serves as both a valuable resource and an instrument. It urges us to calm down, be receptive, and commune with the profound depths of our being. By engaging in the straightforward practice of writing, we have the potential to discover profound understandings that direct our way forward, enabling us to confront the intricacies of existence with increased consciousness, intention, and happiness. As one progresses along the path of self-exploration and personal development, utilize one's journal as a resource, a reflection, and a creative outlet.

Feedback Recursion

As one further explores the practice of developing self-awareness, they come across feedback cycles, which serve as a potent catalyst for personal development and comprehension. This chapter redirects our attention to the exterior by examining how the insights and perceptions of others can function as reflective surfaces, revealing facets of ourselves that may be invisible to the naked eye. When feedback is actively pursued and received with sincerity and purpose, it serves as an indispensable instrument in the process of self-exploration and individual growth.

Characteristics of Feedback Loops:

In the realm of personal development, a feedback loop denotes the reciprocal exchange of information between ourselves and the outside world. This feedback may originate from acquaintances, family members, friends, coworkers, or even casual acquaintances. The determining factor is not the origin of the feedback, but rather its caliber and our preparedness to constructively incorporate it.

Request for Feedback:

In order to establish positive feedback cycles, one must initially engage in proactive feedback collection. This endeavor necessitates a level of courage and susceptibility, as it entails exposing oneself to the evaluations and criticisms of others. Nevertheless, adopting a growth mindset entails perceiving feedback collection not as a means to expose imperfections, but rather as a means to identify prospects for development and enhancement.

When soliciting feedback, be particular regarding the aspects in which you wish to develop, and select individuals in whom you have faith that they will offer candid and constructive criticism. Approaching this process with a distinct purpose in mind is of utmost significance; concentrate on how the feedback can facilitate your progression towards self-awareness and individual growth.

Obtaining Remarks:

Acquiring feedback is a skill in and of itself. It entails attentive and candid hearing, devoid of hasty defense or justification. This can present a difficulty, particularly when the feedback pertains to delicate subjects or areas that are not seen. Nevertheless, the objective of receiving feedback is not to validate our self-perception, but rather to enhance our comprehension of our own being.

Strive to maintain a rational distance between your emotional reaction and the information being conveyed in order to receive feedback. Devoutly contemplate the feedback's validity and the extent to which it corresponds with your personal perceptions and objectives. It is important to bear in mind that feedback is merely a viewpoint and not an evaluation; rather, it can offer significant development-oriented insights.

Consolidating Feedback:

The genuine efficacy of feedback resides in its integration into a practice of self-awareness. This process entails engaging in introspection regarding the feedback, identifying sections that align with our personal experiences and objectives, and devising strategies to integrate this revised comprehension into our behaviors and choices.

Incorporating feedback could necessitate behavioral modifications, communication style adjustments, or a reevaluation of objectives. A process that, despite occasional discomfort, has the potential to bring about substantial development and metamorphosis. By adopting feedback as a pedagogical instrument, we expand our horizons and expose ourselves to a multitude of potentialities, thereby enhancing our process of self-exploration.

Establishing an Environment That Values Feedback:

Ultimately, developing self-awareness via feedback cycles is a relational endeavor as well as a personal one. By providing others with candid and constructive criticism, we can foster a culture of reciprocal development and assistance. Creating an atmosphere that promotes and supports learning and growth requires not only the active pursuit and reception of feedback, but also the considerate and respectful provision of it.

In the process of traversing the intricate terrain of individual development, feedback loops provide an interactive and dynamic avenue to enhance our self-awareness. These individuals push us to transcend our personal biases, to consider alternative viewpoints, and to incorporate these knowledge into our personal growth trajectory. When striving for self-improvement, feedback serves as more than a mere instrument; it is a valuable bestowment that challenges us to develop in ways beyond our wildest imaginings.

Constraints and Incorporating Self-Awareness into Everyday Life

As this chapter nears its conclusion, we pause to contemplate the process of developing self-awareness—a process that has encompassed the examination of emotional intelligence, the profound impact of journaling, and the intricate relationship between feedback loops. Every individual element functions as an essential instrument in the complex endeavor of comprehending one's own nature and navigating the surrounding environment with enhanced awareness and intention. This concluding segment not only summarizes the fundamental aspects of our investigation but also extends an encouragement to incorporate the knowledge and methods of self-awareness into the routine of our being.

Self-awareness serves as a guiding light on the journey towards individual development and satisfaction. Establishing a solid foundation is crucial in developing qualities such as empathy, resilience, and genuine connection. Through the development of self-awareness, individuals gain insight into their emotions, motivations, and the far-reaching consequences of their behaviors on both themselves and others. Although profoundly individual, this expedition embodies universal themes of enlightenment and metamorphosis.

Constant Application of Self-Awareness:

Consciously incorporating self-awareness into our daily lives is not a chore that demands completion; rather, it is an ongoing endeavor—a state of being that enhances each instant and engagement. It requires a dedication to introspection, an eagerness to learn, and a willingness to embrace transformation. In the future, may we retain the knowledge and understandings gained from this chapter and implement them in manners that shed light on our journey and direct our actions.

Adopt Emotional Intelligence: Strive deliberately to interact with one's own emotions as well as the emotions of others in a compassionate and empathetic manner. Strive for self-control and cultivate empathetic, robust relationships in both your professional and personal spheres.

Establishing a Journaling Routine: Consistently allocate time to maintain a journal, utilizing it as a platform to contemplate one's experiences, emotions, and the knowledge gained throughout the process. Utilize your journal as a repository of personal development, a reflective surface for your reflections, and a canvas for your thoughts.

Solicit and Analyze Feedback: Initiate the process of soliciting feedback from individuals in your vicinity and adopt a receptive mindset. Leverage feedback to foster introspection and development by incorporating it into your self-awareness and comprehension of your global influence.

Cultivate a Growth Mindset: Consider each experience a chance to acquire knowledge and develop personally. Embrace challenges, derive valuable lessons from setbacks, and commemorate triumphs as significant turning points along the path to self-awareness and individual growth.

A Request for Action:

In light of the chapter's conclusion, please perceive this as an impetus to implement the principles of self-awareness into every aspect of your existence. Leverage the knowledge and understanding that you have acquired to direct you toward a more mindful, interconnected, and satisfying life. Engage in a daily practice of intentional living, approaching the process of self-exploration with bravery and receptiveness.

Always keep in mind that the journey towards self-awareness is a spiral, not a linear one, in which each iteration yields greater insight and comprehension. Difficulties and moments of enlightenment are inevitable; nevertheless, your dedication to developing self-awareness will serve to illumine your path, enhancing not only your own life but also the lives of those in your vicinity.

By adopting the principles of self-awareness, individuals initiate a profound and transformative process—one that not only results in an enhanced comprehension of one's own being but also fosters a more compassionate, empathetic, and interconnected global community. We must approach this journey of self-awareness with assurance, inquisitiveness, and a dedication to development, for it is through this process that we discover the means to realize our utmost capabilities.

4

Chapter 3: Developing a Growth Mindset

Embracing Difficulties

The foundation of cultivating a growth mindset is a fundamental change in viewpoint: rather than perceiving obstacles as insurmountable barriers, view them as chances for personal development, knowledge acquisition, and exploration. This paradigm shift in our approach to challenges is not merely a personal development tactic; it is an entirely new way of interacting with the world.

Seeing the Potential in Obstacles:

It is by the very nature of challenges to force us to leave our comfort zones. They force us to confront our anxieties, challenge our assumptions, and push us to our limits. Genuine progress is achieved during these instances of unease and uncertainty. Analogous to a seed germinating in the soil, we emerge from adversity more robust, resilient, and certain of our own capabilities.

Nevertheless, accepting challenges is frequently simpler said than done. It could be that our inherent tendency is to desire security, familiarity, and comfort. However, the foundation for development is laid with the cornershow of tenacity and bravery. By confronting obstacles directly, we expose ourselves to the immense capacity for personal growth and change that resides within.

The Reframing Obstacles:

Reorienting one's perception of challenges is an initial step toward embracing them. One may perceive a challenge not as a menace to their expertise or sense of self, but rather as an opportunity to progress. This paradigm shift necessitates the cultivation of mindfulness and regular practice, as it confronts profoundly entrenched thought and behavior patterns.

Please reflect on a current challenge that you are confronted with. By reorienting one's inquiry from "Why is this happening to me?" to "What can I learn from this? How can this strengthen me?" a moment of vulnerability and adversity can significantly modify an individual's emotional reaction to adversity, converting feelings of anxiety and fear into enthusiasm and anticipation.

Confronting Obstacles with Inquisitiveness and Self-Assuredness:

Once our challenges have been reframed, we must now approach them with an attitude of inquisitiveness and assurance. Curiosity enables us to transcend our immediate unease and investigate the potential for personal development and knowledge acquisition. Consisting of a strong conviction in our own capabilities and a solid history of accomplishments, confidence empowers us to proceed with audacity despite the presence of unpredictability.

In order to foster this methodology, commence by establishing modest, feasible objectives that challenge your capabilities. Regardless of their magnitude, commemorate your accomplishments and utilize them as opportunities to develop your self-assurance. Leverage your curiosity in the face of setbacks by inquiring about them and pursuing insights that can inform your subsequent actions.

The Significance of Community and Support:

The process of embracing challenges is most effectively navigated in the company of others. It is advisable to associate with people who exemplify the growth mindset—individuals who perceive obstacles as chances for personal development and motivate you to surpass your own perceived boundaries. Actively pursue mentorship opportunities, participate in communities comprised of individuals who share your interests, and initiate dialogues that expand your horizons and motivate you to persevere.

To conclude, engaging challenges constitutes not a mere element but rather the fundamental nature of cultivating a growth mindset. It is about perceiving each challenge as a valuable opportunity to develop into our utmost potential. We discover a universe of opportunities in which development becomes a mode of being rather than merely an effect as we develop the ability to confront obstacles with inquisitiveness, self-assurance, and the assistance of our peers. It is imperative that we approach the forthcoming challenges with confidence, recognizing that each one presents a chance for personal growth and the potential to achieve our utmost capabilities.

Suffering and grit

Growth mindset principles are intricately interwoven with perseverance and fortitude, which are fundamental and highly dynamic components. They symbolize an unyielding determination and steadfast commitment to persevere despite obstacles and setbacks. This chapter delves into the unwavering determination of perseverance and the profound strength of grit, and how they both contribute to the development of a growth-oriented and resilient mindset.

Fundamental to Perseverance:

Perseverance serves as the latent force that propels individuals to persist in their pursuit of objectives, notwithstanding obstacles, setbacks, or the allure of surrender. It is the persistent effort necessary to complete a task, regardless of how difficult it may be. Instead of a solitary, monumental action, perseverance consists of an innumerable number of minor, frequently unseen choices to continue making progress on a daily basis.

Grit: The Foundation of Success:

Angela Duckworth, a psychologist, defines grit as the fervor and persistence required to achieve long-term objectives. Regardless of how remote they may appear, it is our unwavering dedication to our aspirations and our stamina that propel us toward success. On the path to success, grit is the driving force that propels us through the inevitable trials and tribulations.

Grit and Perseverance Cultivation:

Cultivating these attributes necessitates not solely intellectual comprehension, but also pragmatic, routine behaviors and a paradigm shift. The following are approaches to instilling perseverance and fortitude within one's essence:

Established, Significance-Being Objectives: Grit and perseverance thrive in the realm of purpose. It is crucial to establish unambiguous long-term goals that are profoundly aligned with one's values and passions. Unshakable motivation to persevere can be discovered when one's objectives align with their innermost being.

Embrace the Process: Recognize that the trajectory towards attaining one's objectives is seldom in a linear fashion. Accept every obstacle, impediment, and setback as a fundamental component of the expedition. Develop the insight to derive pleasure from surmounting challenges, as opposed to perceiving them exclusively as barriers to your accomplishments.

Construct an Indestructible Ritual: Construct individualized rituals that assist you in recharging and refocusing in the face of adversity. This may be accomplished through journaling, meditation, or a daily stroll. These practices have the potential to function as a constant reminder of your objectives and the rationales that drive your endeavor, thereby fortifying your determination to persist.

Motivate Oneself: Derive fortitude and inspiration from the narratives of individuals who have exhibited exceptional perseverance and tenacity. The journeys of historical figures, contemporary champions, and members of one's own social circle can provide inspiration and invaluable lessons.

Cultivate a Supportive Community: Establish a social circle comprising individuals who foster your personal development and recognize the significance of tenacity. When your resolve wanes, a community that both challenges and supports you can be an extraordinary source of fortitude.

What Perseverance and Grit Can Accomplish:

The process of attaining our aspirations is replete with obstacles that put our determination, perseverance, and strength to the test. However, it is precisely because of these characteristics—perseverance and grit—those who succeed from those who fail are distinguished. These capabilities empower individuals to surpass their own perceived boundaries, to rebound from setbacks with revitalized resolve, and to persist in their endeavors with a steadfast conviction in their ultimate achievement.

By nurturing these attributes internally, we not only enhance our ability to accomplish our objectives but also fortify our ability to confront the intricacies of existence with poise and fortitude. Beyond mere routes to achievement, perseverance and fortitude serve as declarations of our dedication to personal development, the realization of our aspirations, and ultimately, to the maximum realization of our capabilities. Subsequently, let us resolve to cultivate these attributes internally, as they represent the pivotal factor in unveiling our genuine potential and attaining the magnificence that we are all capable of.

The Function of Positive

Regarding the cultivation of a growth mindset, the significance of positivity cannot be emphasized enough. It is the illumination that guides us through the most arduous obstacles, the mild prodding that uplifts us when we stumble, and the whisper that motivates us to consider the potential for success in spite of our setbacks. This chapter explores the profound impact of positivity on our lives, revealing how adopting a positive perspective not only facilitates personal development but also profoundly changes our approach to the challenges that arise throughout our journey.

Comprehension of Positivity:

Positive thinking transcends mere optimism; it is a deliberate decision, a perspective that recognizes obstacles while centering on prospects and resolutions. It pertains to sustaining a positive perspective on life, having faith in one's own capabilities, and anticipating favorable outcomes. Adopting this perspective is of utmost importance in cultivating resilience, as it empowers us to confront challenges with a sense of determination and potentiality, as opposed to fear and hopelessness.

The Scientific Basis for Positivity:

Positive psychology has demonstrated that an optimistic outlook can significantly impact one's physical and mental health, stress tolerance, and general state of being. Lower rates of depression, improved stress management, increased resistance to the common cold, and even extended life spans have all been associated with positivity. Positive emotions have the potential to induce the development of fresh neural connections, enhance cognitive functioning, and augment mental resourcefulness at the neurological level.

Developing a Positive Perspective:

The development of a positive attitude necessitates deliberate actions and a change in mindset. Listed below are methods for incorporating more positivity into your daily life:

Develop an Appreciation Practice: Establish a routine of introspection and gratitude towards the positive aspects that grace your life. One can greatly improve their mood and perspective by keeping a gratitude journal or dedicating a few moments each day to mentally acknowledging the things for which they are grateful.

Reframe Obstacles: Develop the habit of perceiving challenges as chances for personal development, rather than as overcomeable barriers. Consider how each circumstance can serve as a learning opportunity and how it can aid in your personal growth.

Cultivate Positive Relationships: Create an environment where individuals inspire and provide assistance. Positive social interactions have the potential to significantly improve one's disposition and perspective, offering motivation and inspiration during moments of greatest need.

Participate in Positive Self-Talk: Maintain awareness of your internal monologue and deliberately redirect pessimistic or self-deprecating thoughts towards sentiments that are more constructive or empathetic. Maintain motivation and confidence by recalling your past accomplishments and areas of strength.

Developing an Attitude of Mindfulness and Appreciation for the Present Moment Can Help You Discover Joy in the Small Things. One can become more positive and fulfilled by deriving pleasure from ordinary, mundane occurrences.

The Effects of Goodwill on Development:

Accepting positivity does not entail disregarding the challenges of existence or pretended that every aspect is flawless. Instead, the key lies in embracing a mentality that prioritizes potential and advancement, which facilitates the process of overcoming obstacles and setbacks. Positive thinking stimulates motivation, fosters perseverance, and expands our horizons in search of novel solutions and possibilities.

When striving to cultivate a growth mindset, positivism serves as both the means and the endpoint. It enables us to confront existence with bravery and hopefulness, guaranteeing that notwithstanding the challenges we confront, we maintain an unwavering conviction in a more promising, development-oriented future. This chapter functions as a poignant reminder of the profound impact that positivity can have on our lives; it urges us to wholeheartedly embrace the inner light that guides us as we navigate the complexities of our individual development.

The Importance of Failure

Failure is an essential component of the growth mindset symphony, yet it is frequently misconstrued. It is a recurring motif in the narratives of all those who are seeking for personal improvement. However, these instances of perceived defeat are where the harmony of development, achievement, and ultimate success can be heard. This chapter delves into the intricate correlation between growth and failure, emphasizing the significance of reorienting our viewpoint on failure as a fundamental component in cultivating a resilient growth mindset.

Definition of Failure:

Before we can begin this voyage of transformation, we must redefine what failure entails. Failure, in its conventional sense, is frequently regarded as an indication of demise—a sign to cease one's endeavors. As an integral component of the learning process, failure is not a declination when viewed through the lens of a growth mindset. This is not a reflection of our value or potential; rather, it presents an invaluable opportunity for introspection and reorientation.

Stigmatization of Failure:

Failure is frequently stigmatized by society, which equates it with feelings of humiliation and inadequacy. For fear of failure, this perception may inhibit our willingness to take risks or attempt new things. Overcoming this social stigma necessitates a deliberate endeavor to modify our internal monologues concerning setbacks, acknowledging that the most profound insights frequently emerge from our setbacks and disappointments.

Developing from Setbacks:

Our reaction to failure constitutes its true potency. Each setback and error contains a wealth of information—hints as to what failed and indications of what could succeed. Failure-based learning entails the execution of three crucial stages:

Reflection: Obtain an impartial perspective in order to assess the circumstances. What malfunctioned? What were the contributing factors that led to the outcome? The purpose of this reflection is not self-blame, but rather an awareness of the underlying dynamics.

Lesson Extraction: Determine which lessons are intrinsic to the failure. What have you learned from this experience regarding your strategies, methods, or presumptions? How can your future actions be informed by these insights?

Implementation of Insights: Modify your approach in light of the lessons learned. This may entail exploring an alternative approach, gaining additional competencies, or even adapting one's viewpoint. Implementing these insights in a manner that advances you and brings you closer to your objectives is crucial.

Cultivating Resilience via Adversity:

Developing a mindset that views failure as a valuable learning experience inherently promotes resilience—the ability to recover from adversity with increased strength and resolve. This resilience is a muscle that is developed through repeated exposure to adversity and the application of acquired knowledge.

Developing a Culture of Acceptance for Failure:

Cultivating a growth perspective regarding failure extends beyond individual development and has the potential to revolutionize the contexts in which we function. By fostering an environment in which failure is accepted as an inherent component of the learning journey, whether in the workplace, family, or school, we establish environments where people feel secure enough to venture out, innovate, and ultimately, develop.

Redefining our relationship with failure, in summary, is a fundamental aspect of cultivating a growth mindset. It is imperative that we transcend the immediate anguish of defeat in order to derive insight from our failures and implement this understanding with renewed resolve. By utilizing this chapter as a manual, we can learn to view failure not as a formidable adversary but rather as an instructive force, whose guidance forms the bedrock of our personal development and exploration. By adopting this perspective, we can start to understand that the underpinnings of our previous setbacks frequently serve as the foundation for our most monumental triumphs.

Synopsis and Practical Measures

As this chapter on cultivating a growth mindset draws to a close, we have explored various aspects including the benefits of embracing challenges, the significance of perseverance and fortitude, the transformative potential of positivity, and the invaluable insights that can be gleaned from failure. Every single one of these components is essential in cultivating a mindset that is robust, receptive to development, and capable of surpassing the constraints that were previously perceived as unchangeable. This concluding segment not only summarizes our expedition but also provides practical measures to incorporate the tenets of a growth mindset into our everyday existence.

Embracing the Journey of the Growth Mindset:

The pursuit of cultivating a growth mindset is an ongoing and profound endeavor. The process never concludes with the mere acquisition of knowledge; rather, it commences anew with every practical application of that knowledge. Beyond merely altering our thought processes, embracing a growth mindset entails a fundamental transformation in our way of life, learning, and engaging with the opportunities and challenges that arise throughout our existence.

Practical Measures to Foster a Growth Mindset:

In order to genuinely exemplify a growth mindset, contemplate incorporating the subsequent practices into your daily regimen:

Prioritize growth-oriented objectives that challenge one's capabilities and foster knowledge acquisition. Instead of placing exclusive emphasis on achieving success, prioritize goals that demand the acquisition of novel skills, the investigation of uncharted viewpoints, and the undertaking of actions beyond one's comfort zone.

Engage In Reflective Journaling: Consistently record in a journal your reflections on experiences, particularly those that present difficulties. Utilize this domain to delve into your responses, the tactics you implemented, and the insights you gained throughout the endeavor. In addition to reinforcing a growth mindset, this practice functions as a strategic guide for one's individual development.

It is advisable to proactively pursue constructive feedback from mentors, colleagues, and even critics. It is advisable to adopt a receptive attitude towards this feedback, prioritizing the potential for personal development it offers over any preconceived evaluations or critiques.

Honor Effort Rather Than Outcomes: Reallocate acknowledgment and incentives from the results of one's endeavors to the endeavors themselves. Commemorate the diligence, fortitude, and tactics that you implement, acknowledging that these constitute the authentic indicators of a growth mindset.

Reframe Failure as a Learning Opportunity: Whenever you experience failure, pause momentarily to reframe it as an opportunity to gain knowledge. Consider how this experience may serve as a learning opportunity and how it might shape your future behavior. Fundamental to maintaining a growth mindset throughout the ups and downs of life's voyage is this shift in perspective.

Prompting for Expansion:

In summary, this chapter concludes with a call to action—a reminder that cultivating a growth mindset is an ongoing process characterized by consistent adaptation, learning, and perseverance. The principles delineated herein are not merely abstract notions; rather, they are pragmatic instruments intended to enable you to confront the trials of existence with assurance, inquisitiveness, and an unwavering faith in your capacity for development and progression.

By adopting a growth mindset, one gains access to an infinite realm of potentialities where obstacles are transformed into advantageous circumstances, exertion is regarded with enthusiasm, and setbacks are perceived as valuable learning experiences that lead to accomplishments. Adopting this mentality not only fosters our individual and vocational development, but also fortifies our interpersonal connections and contributes to our holistic welfare.

Let us proceed with fortitude to develop, perseverance to overcome obstacles, and a willingness to gain knowledge from each encounter. We transform not only ourselves but also the world around us by carrying out one growth-oriented action at a time.

5

Chapter 4: Setting and Achieving Goals

A SMART Structure

When pursuing both personal and professional fulfillment, goal setting is comparable to delineating a trajectory on a map. It imparts focus, direction, and a sense of intention. Nonetheless, every objective is not created equal. In order to manifest ambitions into concrete facts, objectives must be formulated with exactitude and lucidity. The SMART framework is a valuable tool that provides direction amidst the frequently ambiguous realm of goal setting.

Preserving Specificity As Your Compass

Specificity is the first principle of the SMART framework. A aim must be precise and unambiguous. Ambiguities that lack specificity, such as "I want to achieve success," fail to motivate individuals to take action. The anchor of your objective is specificity; it clarifies the what, why, and how, rendering your destination obvious. For example, stating, "In order to progress in my professional trajectory, I desire to enhance my aptitude in graphic design," establishes a precise goal and furnishes a robust framework for formulating an action strategy.

Measurability serves as a progress map:

Measurability guarantees that an objective can be quantified. It addresses the inquiry, "How will I determine when my objective has been accomplished?" A goal devoid of a quantifiable result is analogous to embarking on a voyage without a sextant—one cannot navigate or monitor their advancement. By establishing quantifiable benchmarks, such as "Within six months, I will have successfully completed a certified graphic design program," one can establish checkpoints that provide substantiation of progress and invigorate drive.

The attainability of goals serves as a foundation for aspirations:

Achievability of an objective signifies that, considering one's present capabilities and circumstances, it remains feasible to accomplish. Although objectives ought to challenge one's capabilities, they must also be firmly rooted in practicality. Aiming for a star with a projectile is analogous to setting an unattainable objective; doing so will inevitably lead to disappointment and disillusionment. The attainability of an objective is evaluated in order to ascertain whether it is a feasible challenge rather than a pipe dream.

Values Reflected in Relevance:

The concept of relevance verifies that an objective is in accordance with one's overarching life objectives and core values. A objective that deviates from one's fundamental beliefs and priorities acts as an opposing current, perpetually deviating the vessel from its intended course. When one's objectives are in alignment with their genuine values and concerns, they possess a more profound inspiring quality that drives them forward with increased determination and intention.

Time limit determines your sails:

Finally, in order to make an objective time-bound, one must

establish a deadline. A journey devoid of an estimated time of arrival is an objective devoid of a timeline; it lacks immediacy and may induce procrastination. Establishing a specific timeframe for accomplishing a goal instills a sense of urgency that may motivate one to take action.

It is a success strategy, not merely a collection of criteria, that comprises the SMART framework. It converts the abstract into the tangible, and the aspiration into a strategy. You will discover that as you implement this framework to your objectives, your path becomes more lucid, your endeavors become more concentrated, and your successes become more frequent and gratifying. By applying the SMART framework to your goal-setting process, you will be amazed to see your aspirations materialize into accomplishments in the future.

An Analysis of Objectives

Often, the pursuit of lofty ambitions commences with a solitary stride; however, determining the precise location for that stride can present an inherently formidable obstacle. Defining the process of decomposing objectives into more feasible components is comparable to delineating the complex network of routes that culminate in the ascent of a peak. Each discrete undertaking signifies a distinct stage, a critical juncture where advancement can be assessed and drive reinvigorated. This segment explores pragmatic approaches to breaking down ambitious goals into manageable tasks, thereby transforming the pursuit of one's objectives from an unattainable aspiration to a feasible reality.

The Decompositional Force:

Goal decomposition is fundamentally about simplification. An initially daunting objective, such as "composing a novel," is deconstructed into its constituent elements: developing characters, outlining the narrative, and writing each chapter. By means of this decomposition, the overarching objective is converted into a sequence of distinct, tangible tasks, with each task serving as a fundamental component in the progression towards the ultimate goal.

Establishing the Task Hierarchy:

Commence by delineating a task hierarchy, wherein the ultimate objective occupies the apex and a progression of requisite stages enumerates the means by which it is accomplished. By requiring you to consider what is necessary at each stage of your objective critically, this method promotes a more profound comprehension of the task at hand. It involves retracing the route from its starting point to its inception.

Establish Mini-Goals:

Every individual level in the task hierarchy may be regarded as a sub-goal, accompanied by a distinct set of standards for achievement. By employing the SMART framework, these mini-goals are guaranteed to be time-bound, pertinent, specific, measurable, and achievable. By adopting this methodology, the undertaking becomes not only more feasible but also affords consistent occasions for introspection and modification.

The Inspirational Turning Points:

Additionally, objective breakdown functions as a motivational mechanism. The sense of accomplishment and advancement that a mini-goal provides are vital fuel for the long journey toward larger aspirations. These significant achievements serve as occasions for jubilation, signs that one is progressing, and validation of one's capacity to succeed.

Actions of Adaptability:

One crucial element of decomposing objectives is the adaptability it provides. As you advance, you might discover that certain duties require modification, addition, or elimination. Not a disadvantage, but an asset, is this adaptability. It enables you to effectively address challenges and adapt to changes, thereby ensuring that your strategy remains pertinent and in line with your overarching goal.

In essence, the path to success is illuminated by deconstructing objectives. It converts the unattainable into the attainable, and it concretizes the abstract. By breaking down your overarching goals into more manageable and practical measures, you establish a trajectory that is unambiguous, concentrated, and abundant with prospects for advancement. Utilize this approach as a roadmap to successfully attaining your objectives, transforming the formidable endeavor of ascending your peak into a sequence of purposeful, assured strides toward the pinnacle.

Implementing Visualization Methods

Throughout the endeavor of establishing and attaining objectives, the influential capacity of visualization manifests itself as a guiding luminary, shedding light on the trajectory towards fulfillment. Visualization, which involves generating evocative mental images of one's desired outcomes, functions as more than just a hopeful mental exercise; it also functions as a strategic instrument within the framework of success. This chapter explores the profound impact that visualization has on the process of goal setting. It provides practical advice and exercises on how to effectively utilize this influence to render your aspirations more concrete and achievable.

Fundamental to Visualization:

The fundamental principle underlying visualization is that the mind is incapable of differentiating between what is vividly imagined and what is tangible. Engaging in goal visualization induces activation of the identical neural networks that are stimulated during the actual attainment of the goal. This procedure stimulates the brain, synchronizes the subconscious with the conscious, and mobilizes the necessary resources to manifest those mental images.

Developing Your Vision:

Creating a detailed and detailed mental image of the desired result is the initial step in utilizing visualization. This transcends simple reverie and becomes a fully immersive exercise that stimulates all five senses to produce a multisensory, complex experience. For example, if your objective is to complete a marathon, envision the sensation of crossing the finish line, the approving rumble of the crowd, the tactile sensation of the pavement, the tang of perspiration on your lips, and the deep sense of satisfaction that fills your being.

Consistent Visualization Routine:

Embrace the practice of visualization into your daily regimen. Close your eyes for a few moments of solitude each day and become fully engrossed in your vision of achieving success. Engaging in this routine functioned as a daily reaffirmation of one's objectives, thereby sustaining motivation and concentration. These mental rehearsals gradually increase your self-assurance and conviction in your ability to achieve success, thereby rendering your objectives more feasible.

Leveraging Visualization to Surmount Challenges:

Additionally, visualization can be an effective method for predicting and surmounting challenges. While doing so, not only envision the accomplishments but also the obstacles that might be encountered. Envision oneself effectively navigating these challenges by utilizing strategic approaches and capitalizing on intrinsic capabilities. This facet of visualization mentally readies the individual for impending obstacles, thereby diminishing anxiety and bolstering resilience in the presence of tangible difficulties.

Action to Complement Visualization:

Although visualization is a powerful instrument, its efficacy is maximized when employed alongside tangible action. In addition to visualizing your objectives on a daily basis, use the resulting clarity and motivation to take actionable measures toward achieving them. Draw inspiration from your vibrant visualizations to formulate action plans, establish incremental objectives, and diligently strive towards the fulfillment of your aspirations.

The Revolutionary Potential of Visualization:

As you incorporate visualization into your process of goal-setting and accomplishment, you will come to recognize its profound and metamorphic potential. In addition to bolstering motivation and self-assurance, visualization facilitates the synchronization of conscious and subliminal endeavors, generating a synergistic effect that drives individuals towards their objectives. It brings the conceptual to fruition and the unattainable to fruition.

Leverage the power of visualization to illuminate your path to success, using it as a guiding light that transforms the domain of aspiration into tangible accomplishment. By conjuring up evocative images of achievement, one not only envisions the future but also establishes the groundwork for its actualization.

Systems of Accountability and Support

During the extensive pursuit of establishing and attaining objectives, one frequently encounters periods of seclusion during which the way forward is discernibly illuminated exclusively by their own resolve and determination. However, the inclusion of an accountability companion or a support system can greatly increase the probability of successfully completing this solitary journey and convert it into a collaborative expedition. This chapter delves into the critical significance of accountability and support systems in the process of goal-setting. It provides valuable perspectives on how external motivational factors and constructive criticism can act as catalysts for individual development and accomplishment.

The Cornerstone of Responsibility:

Fundamentally, accountability entails the dedication to assume responsibility for one's deeds and choices, guaranteeing that they are in accordance with predetermined objectives and ambitions. When this notion is externalized—when an individual divulges their objectives and advancements to another person—a formidable stratum of dedication is introduced. The external accountability functions as a reflective surface, holding you accountable for your commitments by showcasing your actions (or lack thereof).

Selecting an Accountability Collaborator:

The process of choosing an accountability partner necessitates careful deliberation. This person ought to be someone who is encouraging while remaining firm, and who is both kind and honest. They ought to comprehend your objectives, hold your aspirations in high regard, and exhibit a sincere interest in your triumph. An accountability companion, be they a friend, family member, colleague, or coach, has the potential to greatly enhance one's motivation and commitment to achieving objectives.

Functioning of Support Systems:

In addition to individual accountability partners, external support systems are pivotal in facilitating the attainment of objectives. Mentors, peer groups, online communities, and professional networks pertinent to your objective are all examples of such resources. A supportive community offers a range of viewpoints, motivation, and occasionally the essential resources required to surmount challenges. The combined intellect and vitality of a group can provide encouragement and propel an individual toward their goals even in the face of uncertainty.

Contributing to the Support System:

It is imperative to maintain an active and continuous engagement with your support system. Communicate progress updates, solicit feedback on obstacles encountered, and commemorate milestones, irrespective of their magnitude. Engaging in this interaction not only fosters personal accountability but also strengthens civic bonds, thereby transforming one's voyage into a collective experience. Moreover, by providing encouragement and support to individuals within your network, you strengthen your personal dedication to development, thereby establishing a constructive cycle of inspiration and achievement.

Constructing an Accountability Culture:

Demonstrating a culture that appreciates accountability and support necessitates deliberate efforts. Encourage shared learning, frank communication, and mutual respect. Honor and commend the accomplishments of others as they honor and commend yours. This type of culture not only expedites the progress of individuals but also cultivates a shared sense of development and accomplishment.

Support and accountability operating in concert:

Amidst the intricacies of objective establishment and attainment, the incorporation of support systems and accountability mechanisms into our approach confers a substantial benefit. These elements facilitate the connection between intention and action by introducing an external aspect to our internal aspirations. They serve as an external source of encouragement that enhances our internal motivation, a constructive critic for our thoughts and obstacles, and a support network for our achievements.

By integrating accountability and support mechanisms into the goal-setting process, the expedition becomes a collective undertaking rather than an individual pursuit. It serves to underscore the idea that although our objectives might be individual, the journey towards attaining them does not necessarily have to be solitary. Leverage the potential of accountability and support to illuminate your trajectory, steering you in the direction of your ambitions with a sense of unity, dedication, and common goal.

An Overview and Incorporation of Goal Attainment into Everyday Life

In summarizing our investigation into the process of establishing and attaining objectives, we have traversed the domains of thorough preparation, perseverance, mental imagery, and the indispensable assistance of others. Each of these constituents serves a crucial function in the framework of success, furnishing the support that enables us to materialize our ambitions. This concluding segment not only summarizes our expedition but also provides a road map for incorporating these principles into our everyday existence, guaranteeing that the skill of goal establishment and the methodology of goal attainment become second nature to us, much like respiration.

Embracing the Pathway to Attaining Objectives:

The process of attaining our objectives is replete with opportunities for individual development, revelation, and metamorphosis. This is a voyage that requires perseverance in addition to vision and action, ambition and vision. As we progress, may we incorporate the strategies and insights that were deliberated upon into our daily lives, integrating them into our habits, judgments, and engagements.

Practical Measures for Routine Integration:

In order to incorporate the tenets of goal setting and accomplishment into one's daily existence, contemplate implementing the subsequent practical measures:

Engage in Daily Self-Reflection Regarding Your Objectives: Devote a brief interval each day to introspection regarding your objectives, the advancements you have achieved thus far, and the subsequent actions that must be undertaken. Engaging in this routine on a daily basis serves to reinforce your goals, guaranteeing that your behaviors are perpetually in harmony with your aspirations.

Implement the SMART Framework: Consistently assess and modify your objectives to guarantee that they conform to the SMART criteria, which are as follows: specific, measurable, achievable, relevant, and time-bound. Engaging in this practice promotes enhanced clarity and concentration, thereby rendering one's objectives more feasible.

Deconstruct Objectives into Daily Stimuli: At night, select one to two duties that will contribute to the advancement of your target for the following day. By decomposing objectives into daily tasks, one establishes a feasible trajectory towards achievement, imbuing progress with a sense of attainability and immediacy.

Foster a Supportive Environment: Consistently interact with your accountability partner or support network, exchanging updates, soliciting guidance, and providing motivation. By actively participating, you not only strengthen your dedication but also enhance your personal development through the exchange of knowledge and insights.

Incorporate Appreciation and Introspection: Commemorate each achievement, irrespective of its magnitude, while contemplating the insights gained from every obstacle encountered. Fostering appreciation for the process of travel itself fortifies one's optimistic outlook and ability to persevere amidst challenges.

A Request for Action:

This concludes our concentrated examination of goal setting and attainment; therefore, consider the following a plea for action. Apply the principles that have been discussed in your daily life, rather than treating them as mere chapters in a book. One should approach the endeavor of establishing and attaining objectives with eagerness and dedication, perceiving every stage as a chance for personal development and every obstacle as a testament to fortitude.

Keep in mind that your path to attaining your objectives is distinct and fraught with its own set of obstacles and successes. By incorporating these tactics into your day-to-day existence, you equip yourself with the necessary resources to not only accomplish your goals but also derive pleasure from the process.

Ultimately, the practice of establishing and attaining objectives transcends the goals themselves; it concerns the personal growth that ensues during the endeavor—the identification of strengths, the surmounting of obstacles, and the discovery of delights along the way. Commence the voyage.

6

Chapter 5: Maintaining Momentum and Embracing Change

Constructing Resilience

Within the ongoing discourse surrounding individual development and metamorphosis, resilience emerges as a fundamental pillar—critical, enduring, and empowering. It is our inner fortitude that enables us to persevere through life's challenges, recover from setbacks, and resume our endeavors with renewed resolve. The chapter commences with an exploration of the art and science of cultivating resilience, providing practical strategies and insights on how to strengthen this essential quality within oneself.

Comprehension of Resilience:

Resilience is not an inherent, immutable quality; rather, it is a competency that can be cultivated and enhanced with practice.

Success is the result of a complex interaction between one's mindset, actions, and social support; it empowers people to overcome obstacles, recuperate from difficulties, and adjust to new circumstances. Resilience is a quality that enables individuals to sustain their progress despite encountering difficult circumstances, thereby preventing the unavoidable derailment of their personal development trajectory by life's challenges.

Methods for Constructing Resilience:

The cultivation of resilience is comparable to the establishment of a garden, necessitating sufficient time, attention, and favorable circumstances for its optimal development. The following strategies can be employed to foster resilience:

To commence, it is advisable to nurture a positive mindset and engage in the practice of optimistic thinking. This does not imply disregarding the challenges that arise in life; rather, it entails making the conscious effort to concentrate on what is within one's sphere of influence and discovering the positive aspects in difficult circumstances. A constructive mindset serves as the foundation for the development of resilience, enhancing our capacity to perceive future prospects amidst current challenges.

Embracing Challenges as Opportunities: Rather than perceiving each obstacle as a hindrance, regard it as a chance to develop and acquire knowledge. By adopting a new viewpoint, challenges are converted into opportunities, rendering the voyage not only tolerable but also rewarding. The development of our resilience occurs within the furnace of adversity.

Fortify Your Support Network: The individuals in one's vicinity serve to fortify one's resilience. Develop robust and empathetic connections with family, friends, and mentors who can provide practical assistance, motivation, and insight when required. The awareness that one is not alone in confronting adversity can remarkably enhance one's resilience.

It is imperative to cultivate resilience by consistently participating in self-care practices that enhance one's physical, emotional, and mental well-being. Engaging in self-care practices, such as meditation, exercise, hobbies, or rest, can effectively restore one's energy and alleviate tension, thereby promoting equilibrium and concentration.

Gain Insight from Previous Obstacles and Setbacks: Contemplate past obstacles and setbacks not as sober reminders of lack of success, but rather as instructive instances of perseverance. Determine which strategies were successful, which were unsuccessful, and describe how you overcame those challenges. This process of reflection accumulates a wealth of knowledge that can be utilized to confront forthcoming obstacles.

Strengthening Resilience:

The course of human existence is seldom linear or devoid of impediments. Resilience empowers us to gracefully traverse this trajectory, to recover from obstacles with sagacity, and to persistently strive towards our objectives with resolute determination. Not only does developing resilience involve enduring adversity, but it also entails acquiring the ability to navigate uncertainty and confront each obstacle with fortitude and assurance.

When it comes to sustaining progress and adopting transformation, resilience is an unwavering ally, providing illumination during periods of adversity. Let us wholeheartedly dedicate ourselves to nurturing this essential characteristic, as it is through resilience that we can attain lasting success and realize our utmost capabilities in our quest for self-transformation.

Constant Learning

Throughout the process of individual development, the momentum of ongoing education propels us forward, compelling us to surpass the boundaries of our existing understanding and competencies. Not only is this ceaseless quest for information, expertise, and novel encounters an educational undertaking, but it is also a critical element in maintaining progress and embracing transformation. On a life and in a profession that is constantly changing, continuous learning serves as a compass, ensuring that we maintain our adaptability, relevance, and perpetual enrichment.

The Ongoing Pursuit of Knowledge:

Continuous learning is the understanding that acquiring knowledge is an ongoing pursuit that transcends the confines of formal instruction. Motivated by inquisitiveness, energized by ardor, and directed by the aspiration for development. Each day is an opportunity to gain insight, acquire new skills, and increase our comprehension of the world and ourselves, according to this method of learning.

Developing an Interest in Learning:

Before we can integrate continuous learning into our daily routines, we must first develop an authentic passion for acquiring knowledge. This requires a mental transformation in which learning is perceived not as a burden or a means to an end, but rather as a rewarding and enlightening journey. It entails actively pursuing opportunities for learning in routine endeavors, accepting obstacles as valuable teachings, and perceiving failure as a valuable source of feedback.

Methods for Sustained Learning:

In the same way that we establish objectives for other aspects of our lives, we can find direction and motivation by establishing learning objectives that are both specific and attainable. These objectives maintain the focus and purpose of our learning voyage, whether it be acquiring a professional certification, mastering a new language, or learning a musical instrument.

Diversify Your Learning Sources: Knowledge is more accessible than ever in the current digital age. By incorporating a variety of learning resources (e.g., books, seminars, and online courses), you can ensure that the process remains comprehensive and interesting. In pursuit of insights from diverse disciplines, cultures, and points of view will enhance your comprehension and inspire your creativity.

The assimilation of newly acquired knowledge into one's daily routine is an essential component of learning reinforcement. Attempt to implement what you have learned in practical ways, whether it be in your professional endeavors, personal undertakings, or discussions with peers. Additionally, instructing others is a potent method of reinforcing one's comprehension and expanding one's knowledge.

Embracing change and uncertainty are essential components of the continuous learning process, as they necessitate venturing beyond one's comfort zone. Be receptive to direction changes, experimenting with new approaches, and making errors. Significant growth takes place precisely during these periods of discomfort.

Engaging in consistent self-reflection regarding one's educational trajectory enables one to evaluate advancements, commemorate accomplishments, and modify learning objectives as required. Engaging in reflective practice guarantees that one's learning remains congruent with their ever-changing interests, requirements, and life conditions.

Consequences of Ongoing Learning:

Continuous learning serves as the catalyst for both individual and occupational growth. It cultivates an inexhaustible sense of wonder and curiosity, endows us with the aptitudes required to capitalize on novel prospects, and maintains our adaptability in the midst of change. By making the deliberate choice to pursue ongoing education, we guarantee that our expedition is not merely about attaining a predetermined endpoint, but rather about relishing the terrain of development and revelation that emerges throughout.

On the overarching theme of embracing change and sustaining

progress, ongoing education serves as both the navigational tool and the compass. It provides navigation through uncharted domains, grants access to untapped spheres, and guarantees that we persist not merely as participants but as trailblazers in the expedition of our lives. By embracing continuous learning as a privilege rather than a duty, we can liberate the limitless potential that resides within each individual.

Adjustment to Shift

The personal development process is intricately interwoven with threads of change, producing an inescapable and unpredictable pattern. Devoted to sustaining progress and cultivating development, thus, embracing change is not an option but an imperative. This chapter delves into the skill of adjusting to change—a skill that demands adaptability, perseverance, and a steadfast conviction in one's capability to successfully maneuver through the perpetual currents of change that constitute existence.

A Predictable Occurrence of Change:

The only constant on the path of existence is change. It manifests in an extensive variety of ways, ranging from serene manifestations like the alternation of seasons to turbulent ones like a tempest at sea. Irrespective of its essence, change compels individuals to relinquish the familiar and explore the unfamiliar, thereby exerting pressure on them to surpass their comfort zones and evaluate the extent of their adaptability.

The Mentality Required to Accept Change:

The initial step in adjusting to change is developing the appropriate mindset—one that perceives it not as a challenge to be feared, but rather as a chance for development and acquisition of knowledge. By adopting this viewpoint, we are able to confront change with an attitude of inquisitiveness as opposed to apprehension, to actively pursue the knowledge it imparts, and to utilize those insights as catalysts for our individual and vocational growth.

Methods of Adjustment to Change:

Maintain a flexible mindset: Adaptability is predicated on flexibility. It entails maintaining receptiveness towards novel experiences, relinquishing established routines, and being prepared to modify strategies in light of evolving conditions. Develop flexibility through the practice of mindfulness, which improves one's capacity to maintain present-moment awareness and responsiveness.

Embrace a Proactive Approach: Rather than responding in a passive manner to change, embrace it head-on. Consider prospective changes that may occur in your professional and personal life, as well as strategies for adapting to them. Through proactive preparation for change, one enhances their ability to navigate transitions with increased ease and assurance.

Construct a Support Network: Encircle oneself with people who exhibit qualities of support and adaptability. A robust support network has the capacity to offer direction, motivation, and a feeling of constancy in the midst of constant transition. Furthermore, the act of exchanging personal experiences with individuals who are also undergoing comparable changes can provide invaluable perspectives and tactics for adjusting.

Cultivate Resilience: As previously mentioned, the ability to adapt to change requires resilience. It enables one to recover from setbacks and perceive obstacles as chances for personal development. By maintaining a positive outlook, concentrating on your successes, and deriving lessons from your failures, you can increase your resilience.

Confronting Change with an Open Mind: Ultimately, modify your outlook on change to perceive it as a chance to acquire knowledge, develop personally, and broaden your perspectives. Every alteration, whether anticipated or unanticipated, presents an opportunity to cultivate fresh proficiencies, investigate novel prospects, and enhance one's comprehension of oneself and the surrounding environment.

Accepting Change as a Means to Advance:

Success in an ever-changing world requires more than mere survival; it requires the ability to adjust to change. It pertains to acknowledging that our fortitude is not solely determined by our capacity to maintain the status quo, but rather by our aptitude to progress with poise, resolve, and a receptive mindset.

Permit us to approach the ever-changing terrains of existence with fortitude and inquisitiveness. It is imperative that we perceive every transition as a distinct phase in our continuous narrative of development and metamorphosis. By embracing and adjusting to change, we reveal our genuine capabilities and pave the way towards a future brimming with potential and hope.

In Observance of Milestones

Milestones serve as significant indicators that punctuate our course of personal and professional development. They serve as a reminder of our progress, express appreciation for our endeavors, and invigorate our drive for the future. Commemorating significant achievements is thus not merely a token of appreciation, but an essential custom for maintaining progress and embracing the transformations that accompany our endeavors. The present chapter is devoted to the significance of acknowledging and commemorating progress, regardless of its magnitude, in order to foster a growth mentality and reaffirm our dedication to our objectives.

The Importance of Reaching Milestones:

Milestones function as concrete manifestations of our advancement. They are the successes, both significant and minor, that arise from our commitment and effort. Each accomplishment, whether it be the successful completion of a difficult project, the attainment of a personal objective, or the maintenance of consistent effort, serves as evidence of our determination and competence. When considering the preservation of progress, commemorating these accomplishments serves as a wellspring of delight and drive, strengthening our determination to persist in our trajectory of development.

Acknowledging One's Milestones:

In order to commemorate milestones, one must first acknowledge them. This entails sustaining an awareness of one's advancement and cultivating a cognizance of the instances that merit commemoration. It is simple to disregard the importance of minor accomplishments or to rationalize them as anticipated results of our endeavors. Even though each stride forward may appear insignificant, it is nonetheless a step that merits recognition. We validate our efforts and reinforce the positive behaviors that contributed to these accomplishments by doing so.

Methods of Commemorating Milestones:

Momentum celebrations can manifest in various ways, ranging from modest expressions of self-awareness to communal festivities involving loved ones, coworkers, or acquaintances. A few recommendations to recognize your progress are as follows:

Sharing your accomplishments with others has the potential to enhance the happiness derived from reaching new milestones. Communicating one's accomplishments to others, be it via personal blog posts, social media, or intimate conversations with loved ones, can serve as a source of inspiration and motivation for those embarking on similar paths.

In order to motivate oneself, bestow upon oneself a significant reward upon the successful completion of a specific milestone. This may include a special indulgence, a day off, or an item that you have been longing for. Selecting rewards that align with one's individual values and interests is crucial.

Reset and Reflect: Reward yourself with opportunities to reflect on your journey's milestones. Reflect on your personal development, the obstacles you've surmounted, and the knowledge you've gained.

Subsequently, adopt a prospective mindset and modify preexisting objectives in light of your present aspirations and recognition.

Establish a Visual Representation: Maintaining a visual journal of one's significant achievements can function as an impactful prompt of one's advancement. This may take the form of a scrapbook, digital timeline, or wall chart. Visualizing the accumulation of one's accomplishments can serve as a highly motivating stimulus.

How Celebration Can Help Sustain Momentum:

In addition to signifying accomplishments, the practice of commemorating milestones imbues our voyage with feelings of delight and appreciation. It reminds us that the objective is progress, not perfection. Commemorating significant achievements fosters an awareness of the present, recognizes personal development, and motivates us to confront forthcoming obstacles with assurance and eagerness.

While persisting in the pursuit of our ambitions and objectives, it is crucial that we remember to pause and commemorate the significant achievements that occur throughout the process. These commemorations serve to not only pay homage to our previous endeavors but also shed light on the way ahead, providing us with revitalized energy and a more profound understanding of our objectives. We find the fortitude to sustain momentum, accept change, and continue our journey of ceaseless development and discovery through the commemoration of significant achievements.

A Synopsis and Progressing Towards Change

As this chapter of sustaining progress and embracing transformation comes to a close, we have traversed terrains filled with resilience, ongoing education, flexibility, and the commemoration of significant achievements. Every individual element functions as a guiding light when combined to illuminate the trajectory towards continuous development and metamorphosis. This concluding segment not only summarizes our combined understandings but also establishes the foundation for progressing with change—not as an adversary to be fought against, but as a dynamic collaborator in our pursuit of individual growth.

Anticipating the Path Ahead:

The perpetual nature of personal development is characterized by recurring patterns of advancement, regression, and rejuvenation. This endeavor necessitates not solely dedication to our objectives but also a receptive attitude toward the unanticipated developments that life inevitably introduces. As we progress, may the principles that have been distilled in this chapter serve as guiding beacons, shedding light on our journey amidst the uncertainties that accompany change.

Applying Principles in Everyday Life:

In order to genuinely exemplify the principles of sustaining progress and embracing transformation, incorporate the following practical measures into your routine:

Develop Resilience on a Daily Basis: Incorporate resilience-building practices into your daily routine. Fortify your resilience in the face of adversity by engaging in challenging activities, maintaining a journal, or practicing mindfulness meditation.

Embrace Lifelong Learning: Allocate a portion of your weekly schedule to acquire novel knowledge. Indulge in activities motivated by inquiry, such as attending workshops and seminars, acquiring new skills, or delving into scholarly works.

Maintain a flexible approach to your objectives and plans. Be willing to adapt and modify in response to shifting circumstances, perceiving each change not as a hindrance but as a chance to develop and acquire knowledge.

Regularly Commemorate: Establish a practice of acknowledging and commemorating your advancements. Whether it is recognizing a minor triumph or a momentous achievement, allow these occasions of jubilation to strengthen your progress.

Monitor and Strategize: Consistently assess your advancement, contemplate the lessons you've learned, and devise your subsequent actions. Constant reflection and strategic planning guarantees that one maintains congruence with objectives while remaining receptive to novel prospects for development.

An Appeal to Accept and Appreciate Change:

In conclusion, this chapter urges readers to wholeheartedly adopt change with fortitude, inquisitiveness, and assurance. Unpredictable change presents a fertile ground for development, revelation, and transformation, rather than merely a challenge that must be managed. It challenges us to venture beyond established boundaries, to conceive novel perspectives, and to assume the role of architects of our own future.

Moving forward, let us adopt the perspective that change is a dynamic companion in our personal evolution, rather than a force that deviates our plans. By sustaining forward motion, cultivating fortitude, and remaining receptive to ongoing education, we can adeptly maneuver through the tides of transformation.

Keep in mind, as you enter the subsequent phase of your expedition, that the journey towards development is not an individual one. Bolted by the encouragement of others, driven by the tenets of perpetual growth and adjustment, and motivated by the jubilation of every advancement achieved, you are exceptionally prepared to confront the forthcoming challenges with eager expectation and fortitude. May the insights presented in this chapter serve as a beacon for your continued development, evolution, and acceptance of the boundless opportunities that change presents.

7

Conclusion: Your Transformed Life

Upon Grasping the Journey

As we approach the culmination of this literary work, it is opportune to pause and contemplate the collective journey that we have embarked upon. Having progressed from the preliminary stages of acknowledging our present state of mind to the far-reaching objectives of sustaining progress and imbibing novelty, we have traversed a terrain replete with revelation, adversity, and metamorphosis. This introspection is not solely a nostalgic exercise; rather, it signifies a commemoration of the progress made and the development attained.

The Undiscovered Path:

Our expedition commenced with the pivotal undertaking of acknowledging our preexisting mentality, exposing the convictions and dispositions that have influenced our thoughts and behaviors. This fundamental stage functioned as both a mirror and a window—a mirror that reflected our inner world and a window that revealed the potential for transformation.

We investigated the domains of developing self-awareness and a growth mindset as we progressed. Not only were we to gain a deeper understanding of ourselves through these chapters, but we were also to rewire our approach to the opportunities and challenges of life. It has been comprehended that growth transcends particular domains and concerns, constituting an all-encompassing process that affects every facet of our being.

The Process of Transformation:

Consequently, the methods for establishing and attaining objectives furnished us with the means to convert our recently acquired mindset into concrete results. It was found that objectives serve as more than mere culmination points; rather, they function as milestones in the process of personal development.

Sustaining progress and embracing transformation have surfaced as the ultimate domains of inquiry. We were forced to confront the fact that development is a perpetual undertaking, which demands tenacity, flexibility, and an ongoing dedication to acquiring knowledge. We came to the understanding that although change can be intimidating, it provides the ideal environment for the development of new ideas and concepts.

Implications of the Journey:

Upon introspection of this expedition, it becomes evident that we have undergone a profound transformation. Not only are the objectives attained and the obstacles surmounted significant, but also a paradigm shift occurs in our perception of ourselves and the surrounding world. We have developed the ability to perceive challenges as chances for progress, setbacks as valuable teachings, and development as an ongoing journey.

This change signifies the commencement rather than the culmination. This serves as the foundation for an entirely new way of being and living, one that is adaptable, progressive, and actively pursues obstacles as means to achieve additional understanding and progress.

We should retain in our minds and souls the lessons that have been learned on this journey as we make our way forward. It is imperative that we maintain an openness to the perpetual process of acquiring knowledge, developing, and progressing. It is crucial to bear in mind that the process of personal transformation is not an individual pursuit but rather a communal undertaking, enhanced by the connections we forge and the experiences we accumulate throughout.

We recognize not only how far we have come but also how far we still have to travel by reflecting on our voyage. The forthcoming trajectory is unexplored, and the potentialities are boundless. Armed with the knowledge and tactics we have obtained, we are presently more adept at traversing the terrain of existence, confronting obstacles and embracing forthcoming prospects with bravery, perseverance, and an ever-increasing dedication to development.

Achieved Transformation

As we pause to contemplate the profound voyage documented in these pages, it is critical to acknowledge the change that has taken place. The aforementioned metamorphosis pertains not only to the acquisition of information or the fulfillment of tasks, but rather to a profound shift in our self-perception, understanding of our own capabilities, and perception of the surrounding environment. This chapter aims to expound upon the extent of the accomplished transformation, emphasizing the progression from a fixed to a growth mindset and the far-reaching consequences that this change has manifested in both our personal and professional spheres.

Fundamental to Transformation:

The rationale behind the profound change that we have

experienced resides in the reorganization of our cognitive terrains. Through active application of the principles delineated in this literary work, we have acquired the ability to deconstruct the constraining convictions that previously enshrined us, and in their place, have adopted an empowering conviction in our potential for development and transformation. The transition from a fixed mindset, which regards abilities as immutable, to a growth mindset, which recognizes the boundless potential of individuals, signifies a significant transformation in the way we confront prospects and obstacles in life.

Transitioning from Insight to Action:

The accomplished metamorphosis transcends mere cognitive comprehension and becomes evident in our behaviors and engagements. A growth mindset entails perceiving obstacles as learning opportunities, failing as a means to attain achievement, and receiving feedback as a valuable instrument for personal development. This shift in viewpoint has provided us with the ability to establish more audacious objectives, persevere in the pursuit of our aspirations, and handle obstacles with poise and flexibility.

The Effects on Professional and Personal Life:

The profound consequences of this paradigm shift are discernible in our individual and vocational domains. Within our personal spheres, we have acquired the ability to adopt a positive outlook on change, foster significant connections founded on reciprocal development, and actively pursue our interests with revitalized determination. From a professional standpoint, adopting a growth mindset has empowered us to view our careers as ongoing educational endeavors, seize obstacles as chances for progress, and make valuable contributions to our respective workplaces through our inventive and creative approaches.

An Expanded Viewpoint Regarding Growth:

One of the most pivotal elements of our metamorphosis has

been the realization that development transcends personal accomplishments and encompasses our impact on the well-being of others and our local communities. We have inspired those around us to embrace their potential and forge their own paths of personal and professional development by exemplifying a growth mindset.

Evaluating Accomplishments and Prospects for the Future:

In contemplation of the accomplished transformation, it is critical to recognize the significant milestones attained and the challenges surmounted. Every stride undertaken on this expedition has fostered our development, while each obstacle encountered has fortified our fortitude and sagacity. Anticipating the future, we proceed with the acquired knowledge and the developed mindset, ready to further our personal development endeavors with inquisitiveness, bravery, and a resolute dedication to attaining our utmost capabilities.

In summary, this introspective analysis of the accomplished transformation merits commemoration not solely of the considerable progress made but also of the boundless opportunities that await. The process of personal development is continuous, an everlasting expedition that encourages us to investigate uncharted territories, confront fresh obstacles, and further mold our existence with deliberate purpose, fervor, and an unwavering conviction in our ability to progress.

Implementing Lessons in Everyday Life

As we approach a new phase in our lives, the insights and knowledge acquired during our transformative voyage urge us to incorporate them into our day-to-day activities. By bridging the gap between theoretical comprehension and practical application, this integration guarantees that the values of development, fortitude, and flexibility become inextricably ingrained in our everyday existence. This segment explores pragmatic approaches to ensure a smooth and significant integration, guaranteeing that the resultant transformation is permanent rather than temporary.

Applying the Knowledge Acquired:

The true assessment of transformation is found in the manner in which it materializes in our routine behaviors, choices, and engagements. In order to embody the insights gained, one must adopt a growth-oriented mindset on a daily basis, confront obstacles with perseverance, and welcome transformations with receptiveness and adaptability. The process entails deliberately selecting options that are in accordance with our values and ambitions, thus ingraining the tenets of personal growth in our fundamental selves.

Rational Approaches for Routine Integration:

Commence Every Day with a Specified Intention: Commence each day with a distinct intention of implementing the insights gained from developing and adapting. Your daily intentions should mirror your dedication to ongoing development, whether it be approaching a difficult task with a positive attitude, pursuing constructive criticism to enhance your personal growth, or setting aside time to acquire new knowledge.

Develop Growth-Oriented Habits: Incorporate incremental, growth-oriented activities into your daily schedule to solidify the principles. Potential strategies to foster inquisitiveness include dedicating time for introspection, cultivating an attitude of gratitude, actively honing a particular skill through deliberate practice, or investigating novel ideas and perspectives.

Leverage Obstacles into Learning Opportunities: Consider each obstacle as a chance to implement the knowledge and skills acquired. In the face of challenges, bear in mind the potential of a growth mindset, which entails viewing setbacks as opportunities for learning and individual progress.

Create a nurturing atmosphere by surrounding yourself with people who exemplify and promote a growth mindset. Participate in dialogues that stimulate and impede your progress, pursue mentors who can offer guidance, and foster a culture of learning and development within your professional and personal networks.

Engage in reflective practices at the end of each day, evaluating the extent to which the lessons have been incorporated into one's life and pinpointing potential areas for growth. Maintain a receptive attitude towards modifying your approaches, acknowledging that progress is a continual undertaking that demands adaptability and tenacity.

The Ongoing Process of Integration:

Constantly incorporating the insights gained from personal transformation into one's daily existence necessitates the cultivation of mindfulness, commitment, and a readiness to progress. The voyage is characterized by both moments of success and difficulty, but each provides invaluable prospects for development and enhanced comprehension.

As we progress, may we wholeheartedly and gracefully embrace this endeavor, acknowledging that every day presents a fresh slate on which to construct our development. By imbuing this canvas with the virtues of resilience, adaptability, and perpetual learning, we may fashion a life brimming with vitality, dynamism, and profound satisfaction.

A Call to a Transformed Life:

In summary, the appeal to incorporate the lessons into one's daily life transcends mere invitation; it becomes a responsibility to lead a purposeful existence, to exemplify the progress that has been made, and to persistently pursue the journey of self-improvement with steadfast dedication. Persist in imparting these lessons to others, not merely as recollections of an accomplished voyage, but as operational principles that dictate our actions and impart an enduring imprint of development and metamorphosis onto our existence and the global community.

The Continual Process of Development

The journey of individual development, characterized by the development of a growth mentality, the establishment and attainment of significant objectives, and the ongoing adjustment to change, does not culminate with the concluding remarks of this literary work. Conversely, it introduces us to a vast domain where the process of development endures, a boundless sky that regains prospects for additional investigation, acquiring knowledge, and achieving self-awareness. This chapter underscores the notion that personal development is a continuous endeavor, a never-ending pursuit that forces us to adapt, evolve, and thrive indefinitely.

Accepting Lifelong Development:

The fundamental principle of embracing continuous development is acknowledging that human potential for transformation and progress is boundless. Growth transcends temporal boundaries and is not limited by previous accomplishments or failures. Each new day provides an opportunity for development, encouraging us to employ more expansive brushstrokes, select vivid hues that symbolize perseverance and flexibility, and produce a work of art that mirrors our ongoing progress.

Cultivating an Evolutionary Mindset on an Ongoing Basis:

Maintain Your Curiosity: Curiosity serves as the catalyst for perpetual progress. It stimulates inquisitiveness, the pursuit of novel experiences, and the investigation of unexplored domains. By fostering an intrinsic curiosity, we guarantee that the process of acquiring knowledge and exploring oneself remains a dynamic one.

By embracing challenges as opportunities for personal development, we gain the ability to confront life's obstacles with a positive outlook and fortitude. Every obstacle that is confronted serves as an unexpected opportunity to gain knowledge and understanding that benefits both our personal and professional growth.

It is beneficial to engage in regular reflection as it enables us to reflect on our progress and identify areas that still necessitate improvement while acknowledging our achievements. By means of this introspective practice, we maintain congruence with our fundamental principles and objectives, adapting our trajectory as required.

Develop Significance: It is vital for long-term development to surround oneself with people who motivate, question, and provide assistance. These connections serve as a valuable reservoir of motivation, constructive criticism, and support, infusing our progress with collective knowledge and encounters.

Maintaining a steadfast dedication to lifelong learning is fundamental to achieving consistent progress. It necessitates a steadfast commitment to augmenting our cognizance, abilities, and comprehension, thereby guaranteeing our continued flexibility and pertinence in a perpetually evolving global landscape.

The Inexhaustible Journey of Development:

The pursuit of personal development is an endless odyssey that presents inexhaustible possibilities for augmentation and satisfaction. This is a winding path that traverses peaks and valleys, unveiling fresh perspectives of potential and possibility at each turn. Through our dedication to this endeavor, we wholeheartedly embody the notion of living entirely, engaging with the world with an inquisitive mindset, and making a positive impact with our distinct abilities and aptitudes.

An Eternity Brimming with Potentiality:

We should approach the future with a sense of eager expectation, prepared to seize the plethora of development prospects that lie ahead. By applying the principles and practices that we have examined, we can navigate the intricacies of life with confidence, knowing that our path to personal development is continuous, abundant in possibilities, and constrained solely by our creative faculties.

As this chapter draws to a close, it is emphasized that personal transformation is an ongoing process, not a fixed endpoint. Rather, it is a journey that enhances our lives, fosters a more profound comprehension of ourselves and the world, and motivates us to strive for the utmost manifestation of our being. Let us proceed with fortitude, inquisitiveness, and a receptive mindset, consistently dedicated to the journey of development and the boundless opportunities it introduces.

An Urgent Appeal for Future Efforts

As we near the conclusion of our collaborative exploration of mindset transformation, goal attainment, and embracing the turbulent currents of change, we find ourselves at a critical juncture. The future that lies ahead is replete with possibilities, a broad and inviting horizon that holds the promise of ongoing development, exploration, and metamorphosis. This final chapter serves as a clarion call, urging us to continue the pursuit of personal growth and development in the future. It should illuminate not only our own paths but also the paths of others as we embark on our journey.

Constraints of Our Appeal:

This appeal for action is a declaration of readiness to confront the future with confidence, having developed the necessary understanding, tactics, and fortitude. Living intentionally, integrating the tenets of a growth mindset into each facet of one's life, and maintaining resolute dedication to personal and professional growth constitute a formidable undertaking.

The Transformation in Practice:

Incorporate Growth into Everyday Life: Realize the concepts of growth and adaptability in your daily existence. Consider every day a chance to put into practice what you have learned, to confront your limits, and to venture slightly beyond your comfort zone.

Disseminate Your Transformational Journey: Your personal voyage of change possesses the potential to motivate and uplift others. Please recount an anecdote detailing the obstacles you surmounted, the insights you gained, and the development you underwent. By doing so, one not only strengthens their personal journey but also serves as an inspiration to others.

Embark on New Horizons: The realm of expansion is expansive and multifaceted. Continue to pursue new learning opportunities, challenges, and horizons. Leverage your inquisitiveness to discover unexplored domains in both your personal and professional spheres.

Promote Community Development: Actively participate in the establishment of environments—whether personal, professional, or social—that cultivate development, knowledge acquisition, and receptiveness. Foster support and motivation for individuals in your vicinity as they navigate their personal paths to growth and change, thereby establishing a virtuous cycle of reciprocal development and metamorphosis.

Reflect and reevaluate: Consistently assess your progress and identify novel opportunities for development while taking account of your journey. It is advisable to maintain a receptive attitude towards reassessing one's objectives and tactics, guaranteeing that they continue to correspond with one's progressive values and ambitions.

An Outcome Shaped by Expansion:

The future we enter is a product of our own actions, thoughts, and convictions, as well as the frame of mind with which we confront the world. Through the adoption of growth and transformation principles, individuals not only improve their personal lives but also make positive contributions to their communities and society as a whole.

An Interminable Journey:

It is crucial to bear in mind that the process of personal development and metamorphosis is an ongoing investigation that enhances the quality, significance, and direction of our lives. Let this chapter conclude with a palpable sense of eager expectation and enthusiasm for the expedition that unfolds beyond the confines of these pages.

This future call to action entails an invitation to lead a purposeful existence, to wholeheartedly embrace the continuous process of development, and to establish the principles of transformation as a guiding beacon in our daily existence. As we progress, may we do so accompanied by assurance, inquisitiveness, and an unwavering dedication to ongoing self-exploration, perpetually cognizant of the boundless capacity that reside within us to mold our fates and impart an enduring influence upon the globe.

Appendices

The content of "The Mindset Makeover: 5 Steps to Transforming Your Life" is intended to provide guidance, inspiration, and the necessary tools for a profound personal transformation. The appendices provide practical exercises, suggestions for additional reading, and responses to frequently asked questions regarding mindset transformation in order to further facilitate your progress. The purpose of these materials is to augment your comprehension, refine your application, and respond to frequent inquiries that may emerge during your journey towards personal development.

Practical Exercises

1. **Recognizing Limiting Beliefs Exercise:**

- Write down a list of beliefs you hold about yourself that you feel might be limiting your potential. For each belief, challenge its validity by asking, "Is this absolutely true? Can I think of instances that contradict this belief?"

2. **Cultivating Self-Awareness Through Journaling:**

- Dedicate 15 minutes each day to journaling. Reflect on your day, focusing on moments that triggered strong emotional responses. Explore why these moments affected you and what they might reveal about your underlying beliefs and values.

3. Developing a Growth Mindset Visualization:

- Spend 5-10 minutes daily visualizing a specific challenge you're facing. Imagine yourself approaching this challenge with curiosity, learning from the process, and ultimately overcoming it. Focus on the feelings of accomplishment and growth.

4. Setting SMART Goals:

- Identify a personal or professional goal. Apply the SMART framework to ensure your goal is Specific, Measurable, Achievable, Relevant, and Time-bound. Break down this goal into smaller, actionable steps.

5. Building Resilience Reflection:

- Reflect on a past setback or failure. Write about how it impacted you, what you learned from the experience, and how you can apply these lessons to future challenges.

Further Reading

1. "Mindset: The New Psychology of Success" by Carol S. Dweck

- Explore the foundational work on fixed vs. growth mindsets and their impact on various aspects of life, including education, business, and personal relationships.

2. "Grit: The Power of Passion and Perseverance" by Angela Duckworth

- Delve into the importance of grit and perseverance in achieving long-term goals and how these qualities can be cultivated.

3. "The Power of Now: A Guide to Spiritual Enlightenment" by Eckhart Tolle

- Gain insights into mindfulness and the importance of living in the present moment for personal growth and mental well-being.

4. "Atomic Habits: An Easy & Proven Way to Build Good Habits & Break Bad Ones" by James Clear

- Learn about the science of habits and how small changes can lead to remarkable results in personal and professional development.

5. "The Obstacle Is the Way: The Timeless Art of Turning Trials into Triumph" by Ryan Holiday

- Discover how ancient Stoic wisdom can help us transform challenges into opportunities for growth.

Frequently Asked Questions

Q1: How can I maintain a growth mindset when faced with repeated failures?

- A1: Recognize that failure is a part of the learning process. Reflect on what each failure teaches you and how it can inform your future efforts. Remind yourself of your ability to grow and adapt.

Q2: How often should I set and review my goals?

- A2: Goal-setting is a dynamic process. Set monthly, quarterly, and yearly goals, and review them regularly to adjust as needed based on your progress and any changes in your priorities.

Q3: Can a fixed mindset be completely changed to a growth mindset?

- A3: Transforming a fixed mindset into a growth mindset is a gradual process that requires awareness, effort, and persistence. While tendencies toward a fixed mindset may surface from time to time, with continuous practice, a growth mindset can become your prevailing approach to life's challenges and opportunities.

Q4: How can I cultivate resilience in practical terms?

- A4: Build resilience by developing a strong support network, practicing self-care, setting realistic goals, and learning stress management techniques. Embrace challenges as opportunities for growth and remain open to learning from all experiences.

The appendices function as a navigational tool and schedule for your ongoing process of self-transformation. Permit them to direct you toward a more profound comprehension, more fulfilling experiences, and a life revolutionized by the influence of a growth mindset.